FROM CONVICTED TO COP

FROM CONVICTED TO COP

HOW A CONVICTED DRUG DEALER BECAME A POLICE OFFICER

THE IMPOSSIBLE TRUE STORY AND THE SPIRITUAL WARFARE THAT MADE IT POSSIBLE, PROVING THERE IS ALWAYS HOPE FOR THE HOPELESS.

TONY STEWART

XULON PRESS

Xulon Press
2301 Lucien Way #415
Maitland, FL 32751
407.339.4217
www.xulonpress.com

Paperback ISBN-13: 978-1-6628-3957-3
Hard Cover ISBN-13: 978-1-6628-4383-9
eBook ISBN-13: 978-1-6628-3958-0

Dedication

What a blessed life I enjoy. There is no way I could have written these words if I did not have the family and friends God has given me. I never saw them coming and am so blessed they arrived in my life.

To my wife, Kim: Without you, I could not have survived to write my story.

To my son, Anthony: You are my anchor that does not drift.

To my daughter, Melanie: You inspire me to see beyond the horizon.

To my granddaughters, Jewel, Zoie, and Emma: You have taken up a place in my heart that cannot be measured.

To my grandson, Colin: My heart breaks each time I call your name. At age twenty-one, God called you home. I will love you always, and I will embrace you again one day.

To my Mother In Law, Jewel Henson Lemmons: You are a faithful Angel on this earth.

To my family and friends, you are all my heroes.

This book is mainly dedicated to souls who, like me, have lost much. This includes the families and friends of those who, like me, lost all hope of ever seeing peace. My story proves there is hope for the hopeless.

Table of Contents

Preface

The events that inspired me to write this book all happened. No part of this story is fiction.

The battle to stop this book from reaching you intensified in horrible ways as the day of printing grew close. A car crash took the life of my twenty-one-year-old grandson Colin Kittrell and two other precious teenagers in the opposing car.

Just before that, my seventeen-year-old Clemson University freshman granddaughter Jewel Kittrell came very close to death. These attacks only delayed the delivery of these words.

Before I was fourteen years old, Evil and I had grown so close together that many thought we were one. This enemy called Evil robbed me of much, including my childhood and my mother. On this journey, Evil used its influence to take the lives of many around me while imprisoning and destroying others through addictions and careless living. Victory for me did come, and it did so with no help from me.

For far too many years, I never understood Evil existed at all. I was wrong! Spiritual warfare does exist. It hides in plain sight and convinces us we are the cause of all bad things that happen and that Evil is not a living entity—wrong, very wrong!

Evil thrives through lies and misdirection. If you believe you are predestined to be defeated with no hope of a heavenly home, then you are a victim of a great lie!

If you do not believe in the existence of a living Good or Evil, then read the story of my life as just an entertaining story. Much of this story happened before I believed in anything myself. However, if you keep an open mind throughout this story, you will quite possibly begin to see similar events in your own life or lives near yours. Evidence of miracles and intercessory rescues will be shared. I changed some names and places, but the content is factual! What I thought was a single book has now grown. The losses I wrote about have not stopped. Today book two is planned. It is my inspiration to share how to spot trouble traps in your life before you fall victim to similar evils.

I was known as Evil for many years, and I did horrible things. I became Evil Me!

Hope for the Hopeless

A prime reason for my writing is to alert the hopeless that hope is still possible. The journey to healing starts with recognizing that Evil exists and Good is always nearby and ready to help.

Evil won too many battles against me, but those victories did not last. Violence, hate, rage, and all their constituents became my constant companions, while unseen battles for my future were also occurring. My story will illustrate how I became Evil myself or chose to invite Evil to lead my life, but the misery I was part of was overcome. Today, constant rage has been replaced with enormous peace. The same can be true for you or someone you love. This story provides ways to avoid most of the future *Trouble Traps* and get past lost battles.

I write to promote hope and healing. If I can return from the grip Evil had on me, there is hope for anyone! Follow me on my life's journey if you or a loved one have walked similar roads to the evil ones I have traveled. In this book and those to follow, I tell stories of both horrible events and great victories. Peace and hope can defeat Evil. My story illustrates there is a recipe for a healthier and happier life. Suffering does not have to last throughout a lifetime.

Although we do not create Evil in our lives, it is a fact we open the door for Evil to enter our lives through the people, places, things, and events we choose, but we are not *born* Evil. Evil is a living entity that has been around since the creation of time itself. Evil lives and walks near us. Spiritual warfare will take on a new meaning for you well before you finish this read.

You must also understand we are all good people, and no matter how many mistakes we make or sins we commit, we can still return to a happy and more peaceful life. I offer my story as evidence of this truth.

Some ask why Evil is allowed to exist at all. I am no authority on this, but I am an authority on how Evil impacts our lives. I became an authority through my experiences. I pray you never have to go through such things yourself. At some point, the abundance of evidence in my story will illustrate how a hidden battle is raging. I suggest you accept the fact that the most influential war plans include sneak or surprise attacks. Hidden attacks always work best. *The greatest trick Satan ever pulled on us is to convince the world he does not exist!*

Evil's battle strategy is to attack us without us even realizing he exists at all. If you or someone you care about has fallen deep into his *Trouble Traps*, then this true story will serve to make it harder for him to do his harm again.

Few have fallen further down into the pits of hell than me. But with help, Evil's grip on me was defeated, and I returned to a life of peace and happiness. My writing aims to prove Evil exists and, better yet, to teach you how to return from the losses he has enabled in your life.

This battle cannot be won alone. Find help and carefully pick the people to surround yourself with. The places and things to avoid will become apparent when you read my journey to hope.

The Evil that works against us uses a battle strategy that has been perfected over thousands of years. This evil one also hides very well. Today, you can begin a comeback. Today, you will learn of his hidden strategies and lies. Today, Evil will start to lose its grip on your future. Today, intercession can grow.

If I can return from the horrible places I visited, so can you or your loved one. *There is no evil journey from which you cannot return.*

Reading Tips

will use some terms often that should be explained. I will also take some liberties with capitalizations.

Why capitalize? Often, influences we have always thought of as non-living are Heavenly Agents (Angels) sent to help us or the Opposing Agents (Fallen Angels) sent to harm us by the master of Evil himself, Satan.

Don't believe in such supernatural things? Then look at the evidence I share and arrive at your choice of conclusions. However, the evidence I share will help you avoid similar mistakes in your life's journey.

- If we do not place a new focus on the sources of harmful influences, we will more easily fall into evil *Trouble Traps* set for our demise. Also, other unseen Heavenly Agents can and do facilitate peace and hope while Opposing Agents work to deliver hurt and pain.

Intercession: The act of intervening on behalf of someone else. I cite as the creator of this term, the creator of the universe himself, the father in heaven.

- While some such actions can be in-person through humans, I will also use this term to illustrate that an earthly human prayed to the Lord Jesus Christ to provide heavenly support for me. Jesus himself sent the delivery of this intercession, and he used the wisdom of the Holy Spirit or his Heavenly Angels as the delivery channel.

Ancestral Intercession: Healthy influences on our lives can come from our great grandparents and well before we are born. Today you can start just such intercession by praying for unborn descendants or future generations.

- Ancestral Intercession works because the Lord Jesus wants to respond to Righteous Prayers. Righteous Prayers that ask for future assistance for our descendants are easy for him to answer.

Coaches/Life Coaches: A person who counsels, encourages, and directs us. I will use this title for humans who only offer "positive" advice! Life coaches often have a continued presence in our lives.

- Family members often act as life coaches, but friends and even strangers can take on this role.
- This kind of healthy mentorship is often found in Christian churches.

Crossing Guards: A volunteer who is present and offers directional advice before we take a life-altering turn. Guides at each crossroads can offer good or bad advice.

- We may not notice these guards in real-time.

Principalities and Influences: Many healthy influences in our lives, such as hope, have Angels assigned to them. The same is true for harmful effects like violence and pain. Angels from heaven or hell govern each of these influences. It is also true that places (principalities) are assigned healthy or harmful Angels.

Generational Blessings/Generational Curses: We are all born into one or the other of these environments. If one or both of our parents live a dysfunctional lifestyle, we will most likely adopt some of their unhealthy habits. If both parents live a healthy lifestyle, our chances of making better decisions become more likely.

- It is vital to understand we all can break away from or start such curses. Generational blessings flow through parents and into their children because of the quality of decisions made by the parents. Generational curses can also pour through parents and into their children!

The Trinity: The Father God, The Son Jesus, and the Holy Spirit, all in one. God has shown himself in three ways: God, who created us, loves us, and cares for us; Jesus Christ appeared in human form to make it possible to spend eternity with him, and he is always with us in Spirit form once we accept Jesus Christ as our Savior.

Charts: I believe in making lists. Our lives are so filled with traffic that it becomes easy to miss important events. Evil often slowly delivers attacks. Placing a growing list of good and evil influences on your refrigerator door is a visual way to keep track of your blessings and curses.

My charts show Good and Evil using a point system. It also "Sums" the growing gains or losses. In my story, Evil had numerous and continued gains. Using a point system, I could see where he attacked easier. Slowly, my chart began to show less loss and a final gain.

The Enemy's Objectives

Realizing a campaign existed to destroy my family led me to create an overview of the strategies and objectives used against me. This review is my analysis. Sadly, it was too late to avoid losing some battles. On the other hand, the war was *not* won by the enemy! Better yet, the wounds from lost battles have healed.

At the beginning of all wars is a planning session. A who, what, when, where, and how plan against us always exists—always— and knowing this can reward you with less loss.

- What does the enemy want to capture?
- Who can slow or stop the captures of the desired territory?
- Who are the target's allies?
- What are the strengths of the enemy?
  - Does the evil army leader fear the strengths and influence we have? Does he fear that our positive impact on others might impact his plans?

Below are the enemy's plans for my family. There were and will continue to be new plans.

The Targets

- Betty Gambrell Stewart, born 1928
- Harry Stewart, born 1923
- Tony Stewart, born 1953
- Unknown brother, born circa 1948

1959, Rio De Janeiro, Brazil
Betty Gambrell Stewart, Harry, and Tony Stewart

Evil's "Probable" Mission Statement: Evidence exists that the families known as the Gambrells and Stewarts residing in and around upstate South Carolina, USA, have a history of strong moral principles that must end.

- Each family had praying ancestors in England, Scotland, Wales, Ireland, and recently in the United States, who have asked for intercessions for their future generations. This practice is a threat to our plan to destroy their positive influence on others in the future.

Objectives: Target family member Betty Jean Gambrell Stewart and remove her as a threat to the kingdom of Satan. This battle began at the date of her birth in 1928.

- Reduce or eliminate any healthy influence she has on those around her and especially her husband and children.

God's "Likely" Response Plan

Mission Statement: Protect and strengthen targets Betty Gambrell, her husband, and all her descendants. Turn losses into victories; regain and repurpose captured resources.

Base Line Evaluation: In my story and yours, it is essential to evaluate where you are at the moment and how you got there. Please have patience with me as I write the details of my baseline. My miraculous life stories will begin with the chapter titled The Loss of My Mother when I was Nine.

The Future; What I thought was one book is now three or more. The continued battles in my life have given me a passion for continuing to reveal the enemy's evil plans against us all. Roadblocks in our lives often indicate an attempt to slow or stop us.

Evaluating Our Journey through Life

I t is undoubtedly true we make our own choices, bad or good. One misstep can lead to many more, and soon we become lost in our journey through life. This path of mistakes happened to my mother and continued into my life's journey and my father's, but this did not have to become an endless series of errors for me. The same is true for you.

There came a time in the early years of my life when I was convinced my past would govern my future. More specifically, I lived through so many horrible times I came to believe the rest of my life would continue as before. This thought was a great *lie*! No matter what the past, your future can change.

As I evaluated the troubles the three of us encountered, I realized this path looked a lot like a battlefield. The battles we encountered were often hidden ones with a never-ending barrage of combatants. Besides the mistakes we make ourselves, there are other enemies to fight all along our journeys. Often, we do not know of their influences, and loss is the result of such stealth.

Allow me to evaluate phases of our family's life story as if a war plan was in place against us, and you, too, may see some similarities in your journey.

If I were a commander of an army involved in a war, the walls around me would be filled with charts and maps. So, l used and will continue to use similar tools to evaluate the battles against my family and me.

I will use charts and place a point value on each entry. Ten is the strongest influence (whether good or bad), and zero is minimal.

Some columns may contain more than one person's total, with each being a maximum of ten. For example, two people may share the influence of violence. One is minor (three); the other is major (ten). The sum would show as thirteen.

- On each chart, I will summarize battles and give each a point value. An overall Good versus Evil total will be shown.
- Influences may be grouped. For example, diversions and lies may be a part of an overall battle to distract. In this case, a distraction is often used to cause us to miss another attack. In other fighting, lies may be the leader of the attack to distract us from the truth. In any war plan, there are many variations of the grouping of resources. How these are used varies extensively.
- No two war plans are the same. Evil's strategy to "break us down" can be hidden and take years to do its damage or come at us all at once. While my battle summaries will never match yours, the enemies sent against us often have the same characteristics. Another difference will be that choosing the wrong places, people, and habits will always be customized to each of us.

The heavenly and earthly soldiers of Good and their objectives are often more straightforward. Stealth and hidden goals do not hold the same significance as they do with the evil army.

Also, note that each evaluation may focus on support sent our way from both heavenly and human interventions. Much of this mediation was in the background.

Lastly, don't let the "point spread" lead you to believe the war was lost. Quite the opposite! A lost battle often makes us give up before the final match is decided. That is the ultimate plan of the evil Satan. He wants us to give up all hope prematurely.

There is always hope for the hopeless!

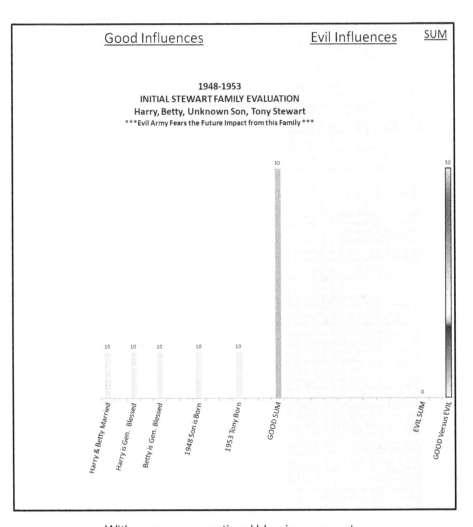

With so many generational blessings present, a prolonged attack is predictable against this family!

Unlikely Outcomes: Convicted Drug Dealer Becomes Police Officer

indeed became a police officer after being convicted as a drug dealer and spending time in jail. How was it possible to clear my past criminal history of these charges to become a police officer? The answer is why I write: *intercession!*

This impossibility was only one in a long list of miraculous rescues sent my way. More importantly, similar recoveries are sent to all of us. Learning to spot and capitalize on them is worth reading this book.

If someone you care about is living a defeated life as I was, this story will open the doors you need to reach them. This journey of hope starts with understanding. Learning how Evil plans to destroy you or the person you care about will open the door to eliminating the "cause" of the problems. Hope grows when we quit focusing on the "symptom" alone and realize the "cause."

If you are a child of a generationally blessed family and were not born under a generational curse, I ask you to accept the fact that dysfunctional lives do exist and are fueled by poor or no parental influences. I was born under a generational curse that came from both parents, but today, I am blessed and no longer cursed.

My story is a success story that those with both generational blessings and curses should read. There is not only a good ending; there is also a miraculous ending! It also includes happy endings for both of my parents.

Before I write of the horrible Evil I have participated in and the resulting intercessory miracles that came my way, let me speak of happier and more helpful things. Yes, I was a convicted drug dealer with time spent behind bars more than once, but after that, I was a Greer, South Carolina, police officer for fourteen years with a completely clean record. This miracle was not the most fantastic thing that happened to me. This story goes much further than this one miracle. The peace that came after my many "rescues" is worthy of your time.

Tony and Kim Stewart, 1991

When I was ten years old, experts diagnosed me as incapable of learning like other children. However, since 1995, I have been a consultant on smart house technology. This role has included travel to over forty states in the USA and four foreign countries. Experts also suggested I be committed to a home—permanently! The "experts" were wrong. Evil must have feared my future. The battle against me was lost!

Too many of us who have lost much give up far too quickly!

I share this story for those who have suffered similar things as I did and then gave up on ever being happy. I write to share how it is *never* too late to return to a life of peace and joy. If I can come back from the Evil that drove me into the pits of hell, anyone can. I have done horrible things, not only to other evil people but also to those caring souls who loved me. I became the best at being the worst, and I lived that life for far too many years. I know the Evil named hopeless. I know him intimately, and I know the faces of many of the other soldiers in his army of misery.

How I came back from the wrong turns I took at each cross-roads required help. Where to find help is what fuels my passion today. Many give up on ever finding their way back once they've made only a few wrong decisions, but hope is nearby, and finding it begins with realizing Evil is a living entity with your name on its hit list!

Before our birth, there is a plan for each of us, full of peace and joy. If we drift off course because of mistakes we make, we can get back on track. There is no punishment pre-planned for us if we make wrong turns. We create our penalties by the pathways we choose to follow, places we decide to visit, and people we allow to misguide us away from hope. Blaming the Creator of hope when we choose the wrong destinations is a mistake. It blinds and leads us to make even more mistakes.

Remember this: *You can often measure the trueness of your life's path by the amount of opposition to it!* Evil sees our potential for happiness more than we do and works to keep us from using or ever realizing the blessings planned for us. Opposing Agents often attack hardest those with the brightest possible future! The Opposing Agents I refer to have evil intentions. Thus, I say again; you can measure the trueness of your course by the amount of opposition to it.

By reading this story, you will fully understand what this means. I can *always* find something special in every person I have met who is living a defeated life. Hidden deep inside us all is always a spark of extraordinary talent that can bring happiness to others. This fact led me to understand why Evil visited so many of us. Could it be that Evil itself did not want our lights to shine? This fact is the truth.

The master of Evil also sees down the road to what our children can become and works to rob the world of what they will do to share hope, love, and peace with others. Evil fears our future and works the hardest against us when we move toward the blessings planned for us and our future generations.

Great distractions visited me to stop me from writing my journey from Evil to peace. I learned that *distraction* is the name of a soldier of Evil that often worked to stop me from writing. He used many distractions, some of which even masqueraded as good things. Success was a tool he often used. It took me a long time to realize success can also be a powerful distraction, maybe even one of the worst! Success also handcuffed many wealthy and famous people I met while consulting on their smart house systems. Success can be an excellent resource for good but can also fool us into thinking we can control our future with no help from anyone or anything else. This untruth is constant and a *lie*! Liar is the name of a potent Opposing Agent.

Living in an orphanage when both birth parents were still alive was one of the few good things that happened in my youngest years. Later, after leaving the orphanage, I will tell of infidelity, sexual abuse, hunger, injuries, and more—all before I was nine years old.

One cold day, injury came to visit and brought the pain of cold and the Evil of disregard to join him. While hungry and locked outside, I jumped off the porch and onto a board with a nail sticking out. It completely penetrated through my foot. Mother and the strange man inside would not come to the door. My cries for help and from the pain went unanswered. That day, new companions of Evil came to take up residence in my life.

That day, I learned what being alone was. Separation, isolation, and many other invading soldiers arrived and would become my constant companions.

How to pull a nail out of my foot myself was also learned the hard way. Pain added his lousy name to my list of companions. I learned to accept these influences at an early age. I also learned these lessons from experience, not from the coaching against such things.

Hiding the cause and location of this injury from my father fueled the removal of parental influence from my life. That lesson introduced me to the Opposing Agents of lies and deceit. Infidelity would also accompany me often. Hunger also visited while Mother and I were outside our own home.

It is vital to note that both my parents were born into generationally blessed families. The influence of Evil turned them. This "turning" is the goal of the evil Satan himself. For a time, It worked on my parents. It also turned me into an "Evil Me" early in my life.

We are not born as cursed. No matter what our parents are, we are born with a clean slate. Sadly, our parents can affect us, and then we can affect others. Such a strategy is the plan of Evil for our world. *Evil is not from our Creator*, who is the doorway to healing and hope.

Such were many of the battles fought in my earliest crossroads. One terrible thing brought with it another. Soon, the evil army overwhelmed me. It would be foolish not to realize such an attack exists. That is the plan of the hidden leader of such Evil. He often uses stealth.

These may seem like significant battles, but they were not. More were to follow, and the strength of those soldiers would be yet more powerful. In 1963 when I was nine, I watched my mother overdose on heroin. It took her life.

In 1973, I was convicted as a violent drug dealer and spent time in military prison and several civilian jails. Evil sang a victory song and celebrated—but it was a premature celebration.

During those days, I partied through an average of $5,000 a week on cocaine and many other drugs. How was this possible? Evil helped, and he invited other troubled souls to join with me. He often sent a party to help me fall. With his help, I also became violent, physically hurting many and intimidating many more. I did this in an attempt to coerce others to obey the voices of the Evil I was following. Some of my closest friends died along the way. I became a leader of the lost. Evil and I often joined forces, and soon I achieved a high rank in his poison army. Sin not only came to visit, but I also became a living evil. You will surely agree how at this stage of my life, I had indeed become Evil Me!

Evil has a lot of allies. Constant negativity and rage were only two of his Opposing Agents, and they soon became my constant companions. Know that today, however, I am at peace, and I have been drug- and alcohol-free since 1983. Not even wine or pain killers have attacked me and won. You, too, can win this battle by learning of the Opposing Agents sent to rob you of hope. This new knowledge should and most likely will make you mad enough to fight back!

My story illustrates the power of intercession. You will discover you can become an intercessory agent for others. You will read about sad and lonely times as I tell my story. You will read about horrible things, but unmeasurable peace and joy did come, can last, and is eternal! Never lose track of the fact we can replace this Evil with peace, love, hope, and joy. My story proves this.

The Loss of My Mother
When I Was Nine

efore wars start, goals are set, and an assessment of the target's strengths is completed. Studies are done to predict timetables, and milestone dates are set. The plan to kill my mother succeeded, but that did not signal the end of the war.

Before my mother's tragic death in 1963, I had already lost the joy of being a child and had grown accustomed to the dysfunctional first nine years of my life. Being a child of a dual generational curse meant nothing to me. Instead, I only knew the lifestyle I was forced to follow. The abnormal was my normal. I did not know I was missing anything.

Many years later, I would compare my childhood to the childhood I wanted my children to experience and realized I must not lead them as my mother led me.

Good and healthy things I would learn of years after her death were not remembered as experiences I ever had with my mother. While I am confident the joy of youth was sometimes present, I had few memories of such things. How was this possible? How could I overlook such things for my first nine years? Today, I know this was and is the plan of the enemy—to rob us at an early age. The strategy was to imbed a dysfunctional lifestyle into me before I ever saw the opposite.

In my early years, complacency fooled me into accepting my surroundings as normal. What else could a nine-year-old with no history of other living conditions think? I thought my abnormal life was to be my everyday life! Being comforted in my mother's lap is not a memory I have. I did not know such comfort even existed. Comfort is a by-product of love. It would be after my mother's death when I was introduced to real love.

My lifestyle while accompanying my mother to the wrong places we traveled was done without my father. He made a home for us and always stood ready to welcome us back, but my mother and I often left home accompanied by the Evil I would only recognize years after her death.

Dad led a lonely and defeated life during those years, but he never gave up on my mother. His love for her frequently came with forgiveness.

The Evil Mother chose to accompany us would become familiar to me. These enemy soldiers wore the faces of men my mother chose. I do not remember a single name or face of these men. Instead, I know them by their evil deeds. Adulterers and sexual predators were common. Addicts whose lives were ruled by alcohol and drugs were also frequent companions in my youngest years.

I don't remember violence as the face of one of these enemies. I can only guess my mother shielded me from such danger. However, the evil soldier named violence did root himself into me at an early age. I know this because of one evil deed I did while in the third grade. After school one day, I knocked a boy to the ground and beat him.

From where did that Evil come? It was never a trait I saw in my mother or father. Nonetheless, it was nearby, and that day, it took a hold on my life I that would use to hurt others at future crossroads of my life's journey!

After my mother died in 1963, I moved in with my grandparents and started life over. The soldiers of my childhood were not welcome in my new home. Hope grew! But the war against me was not over. My evil companions were not ready to leave me alone.

A new phase of the war against my father and me was about to begin. It would also include my battles against my new caregivers and those asking for intercession for both of us.

Immediately after this move, I was tested and evaluated as incapable of ever learning like an average child or taking care of myself as an adult. Committing me to a home for life was discussed. This diagnosis was but one of the many life changes ahead. Changes were about to gain speed.

Before age ten, I agree I was undoubtedly a severe disruption in my third-grade class, but was sending me for testing the best plan? Who did this testing, and which side of Good and Evil were they on?

My grandparents and the school principal disagreed with the advice of these "experts." Instead, they spared me from the destination the experts suggested. This battle against me was defeated by the interactions of those who cared about my future.

Instead, my grandparents introduced me to their home, which was a true haven of peace. They hoped to start me on a different life journey. Out of my sight, a battle was underway for my future. Evil was opposing hope, but hope was slowly growing. Disruption became a major enemy, and he would flex his muscles against me for years to come. Distractions also were everywhere, but hope also had many allies.

I was learning new things other children knew as "normal" since their birth. Although I got a late start on these life lessons, a plan was in place to change my generational curses into blessings.

Each of the following years has a story, but let's race through a summary of the next few years before those battles and victories are detailed.

Until my eleventh year in school, I proved to those experts who predicted I would be a problem in school to be correct. After failing the tenth grade, I took the GED test and entered the United

States Air Force at seventeen. After boot camp, I tested for their special forces unit, pararescue (referred to as PJ), and became the youngest airman to be accepted into their indoctrination program.

I planned to fuel the agent of misery known as violence with this desire, and I moved in that direction for a time. Another future was intended for me, however, and the miracles that made this possible are the reason for this story.

As a PJ in training, I pushed my body and mind beyond their limits, and my combat skills grew immensely. Violence smiled. However, instead of rescuing soldiers behind the battle lines and killing the enemy as a PJ, an injury put me into USAF electronics school. This course would become my lifelong career path. At the time, I saw not being an Air Force PJ as a catastrophe, but there was another unseen plan for my future. Hope was planning to defend my future. The enemy named distraction had lost a battle against me, but I did not see it that way for many years. Instead, I saw a career in electronics as a curse. I was wrong!

As a consultant on smart house technology, I advise new installations and solve problems with existing systems. Not bad for someone with a GED and labeled as incapable of ever learning like ordinary people. I share this to illustrate that yesterday's diagnosis does not have to rule your future. *There is never a journey to a bad place that hope cannot reverse.* The same is true for us all! Evil shrinks when hope grows—always!

As I began a healthy career path, the Evil of my past did not loosen its grip. With a bright future on the table, my old enemies returned to attack me with their well-known temptations and some unexpected new ones. I fell victim to these traps. I now know the hidden enemy suspected the trueness of my path in life would one day make a difference in the lives of others, and he put into place a plan to divert my journey and tempt me down other paths. Diversion often attacks when he fears our course will see a peaceful and prosperous future.

Those enemies won some battles but would lose the war. Diversion joined distraction in their goal to destroy me. Temptation also grew among the ranks of the evil army attacking me.

Evil used an old ally named loneliness to lure me into the companionship of what I believed were healthy friends. Soon, drugs and sexual Evil returned to my lifestyle. I had early experiences with these enemies. Their hurt was deeply rooted in me.

Loneliness came and stayed with me for many years to come. When I traveled with my mother to hurtful destinations, I never knew loneliness. Still, he planned to become one of my constant companions and was always hiding nearby, waiting for an open door into my life.

A new and mighty soldier of violence soon joined the evil army. I became very good at being extremely bad. My PJ training made me even more capable of being physical with my violence. The evil enemy of distraction was working overtime to stop me from ever finding peace. A new and potent enemy named rage moved in. This enemy went to work building more muscular walls in his home inside my heart. His fortress maintained a strong presence and lashed out through me at the worst and most damaging times.

Evil robbed me of knowing of his attacks far too many times. His goal is always to keep us from knowing when something needs fixing in our lives. We must understand what's broken if we are ever to have hope of resolving it.

My goal for sharing my story is to heighten your awareness of the hidden attacks against us all. Violence and rage are examples of Opposing Agents who do not hide, but many secret agents hide their Evil against us and cause us to blame ourselves for mistakes made. Distraction, diversion, and many others are always nearby, hiding in the shadows, ready to silently pounce. Stealth is their strength, but knowing their tactics is wisdom.

After moving into my grandparents' home, my life's journey was taking both good and bad turns. I chose to embrace the wrong turns more often than not, but another unseen force was also at work. The force of Good was fighting for me. Miraculous intercession became common. People were standing nearby, ready to guide me to happier places. Spotting these helping hands took me a while, and all too often, I only saw them after I pushed their hands away, but slowly, the wrong turns I took improved. Intercession was the reason. Sadly, it would be years before I understood what intercession was!

Much of the enemy's plan against us includes an attempt to keep us from knowing about intercession. *The definition of intercession is to pray, petition, or request in favor of another.* I was distracted from knowing intercession existed.

Another critical point to understand is how distractions are vital if Evil is to keep its grip on our throats. Distraction also invites his partners of diversion, division, and destruction to work overtime to achieve his goals.

Hope is a prime target for Evil. Once we stop hoping, we fuel the downward spiral of misery. The evil war general who sends his armies to attack us has a goal of destroying us slowly and subtly. He is proficient at shooting from the shadows and keeping us from even realizing there is a war plan against us.

He also works to make us believe the mistakes we make are permanent, and there is no way back to a place of peace and hope. I did physical damage to people and property. Some of it was beyond horrible. While we can't always fix damage done, we can build a new foundation and begin again. Peace can come again.

The hidden evil enemy has a name. It is Satan. He is a Fallen Angel who robs us of all hope, and he is very proficient at his job. Read more in the Bible in Isaiah 14:12.

Hiding his Evil while it destroys our hope is only one of his planned attacks. Fighting him alone is not possible. The best we can do is recognize he exists and wants to destroy us and stop or damage those who choose to help us. Yes, we make mistakes, but he also sets *Trouble Traps*. We need help, and we need intercession. None of us can do this alone. None of us are strong or wise enough. We all need help!

Somewhere he snuck violence into my life and used that Evil to influence me to push that third-grade friend to the ground and hurt him. While I do not remember violence before that day, he hid nearby and waited for the right time to attack. Evil like this started with someone I encountered, spread to me, then slammed my third-grade friend to the ground. I wonder how his life turned out? Did my Evil that day affect his future? From what I know about the desires of the evil one, I can say with sadness, it probably did.

My story will teach you how to spot the *Trouble Traps* that this evil entity puts in front of you. It will teach you how to pick which crossroads guides and life coaches to listen to when making decisions about your life's journey, and you will learn how to surround yourself with people, places, and wisdom that add protection. You can also know how to ask for intercession through others.

Blessings beyond measure are available for each of us. Stealing them from us is also a goal of the evil one. This annoys me, and I hope it does the same to you!

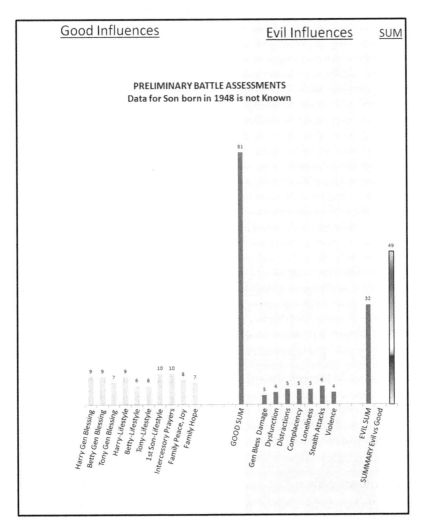

PRELIMINARY BATTLE ASSESSMENTS
Data for Son born in 1948 is not Known

Evil has begun his campaign to reduce or eliminate
this family's positive impact on others.

My Judgment Day at the Greenville County Courthouse

In 1973, I became a convicted drug dealer. I sold PCP to an under-cover agent (who was *not* evil). Time in military and civilian jails followed.

At this point, giving up and giving in would have been predict-able. I decided I had no hope for a better future. The enemy who had attacked me since my birth celebrated.

Fast forward to the year 1992.

My second round of drug trafficking trials was at the same place as my first one in 1973. Even though numerous of the same enemies who had defeated me before were once again present, something was drastically different this time.

Looking back on my mistakes has taught me a lot about things to avoid in the future. The more damage done, the easier it is to see where I made poor decisions. However, on far too many occasions, the attacks were subtle and difficult to identify. Today, though, in this courthouse, I will have some time to review my previous losses.

The subtle evil influencers of my past were satisfied to plant their seeds of Evil in microscopically small portions and then spent years infesting me with unhealthy habits and beliefs in the process. Such a plan often resulted in me adopting bad practices and poor habits, and then Evil fooled me into thinking it was a natural part of my being. Complacency can take its toll on us all.

Searching through the history of the train wrecks of yesteryear was much more accessible, and it led me to ignore the search for the less obvious attacks. Once I began to question the damaging turns I took, I learned how danger stood ready to destroy and was often hidden in the shadows. It was not always a roar that warned me. Often, there was no noise of danger at all.

For far too long, I resisted the notion my choice of friends could be harmful to me. Those people I chose to surround myself with were often my enemies, and I constantly fought to keep them by my side. I now know it is wise to be less eager in calling an acquaintance a friend. I now see how misery *does* love company, and this enemy breeds complacency.

Complacent is always the name of an Opposing Agent. There is no angel of good named complacency!

There were many instances when I surrounded myself with poisonous friends who helped me feel confident that poor decisions were healthy. In addition, I have learned how *not* making a decision can also be harmful. Confusion and indecision breed complacency. They combined to cause me to avoid making positive choices. Confusion often joins complacency in the battle to destroy us. There are also no Agents of Hope named confusion!

My Second Drug Trafficking Trial

The more things change, the more they remain the same. I was right back in the same building where I was judged for trafficking drugs in 1973. This time, it was 1992, and I was once again waiting for my drug trafficking trial to begin. That Greenville County South Carolina courthouse had the same feeling of finality back then, and the waiting room this day had the same worried looks. If I looked hard enough, I could even see some of the same facial expressions. The clock on the wall was running much slower than when I was first here. But this time, my heart was beating much faster.

Strangely, the Evil called confusion was not distracting me this time. I could see yesterday much more clearly.

As was the case during my first visit here in 1973, some of those awaiting trial wore their best clothes while others made a point to wear clothing intended to send a defiant message to the judge. I saw shirts with pot leaves on them and advertisements for beer brands. Most of us waiting for our moments of judgment did not dress to impress at all. The lack of respect for authority was so thick you could feel it without looking at a slogan on a shirt. Lack of respect was another sneaky enemy. I could see from where his energy came. His presence was robust in this room. I even heard him bragging about his disrespectful feats. Sadly, he used the voices of his victims around me.

I did not understand this careless behavior in 1973, and I did not understand it that day. As for me, I felt the weight of every step taken in this room as if it were the final mile. I was intimidated by this atmosphere and sure wished I could be somewhere else. But, here I was again. That day, I would trace the footsteps of the past that brought me to these crossroads once again.

It was not our first time here for many of us in this room, and we were painfully aware that this day would be a long day of waiting, with plenty of time to think about those crossroads where we took wrong turns. We would also remember people along the way who influenced our crossroads decisions. Although I have led the life of a tough guy and often took the wrong path, this day, I was dressed in a suit and tie—no beer slogan shirt for me. No sir, that day, I wanted all the breaks I could get. Disrespect would not win a battle against me that day.

One by one, we would all stand in front of the judge. Some of us were already incarcerated, and others were out on bond. Each of us would all get our turn with judgment that day! Some of those around me could go away for a long time under the habitual offender act. That day, the new name for the repeat offender act is "enhanced offender." However, none of us felt enhanced that day.

Some of the long faces around me were at the beginning of their criminal career and could get smaller sentences, maybe only probation. This uncertainty forces some to pace the hall while others act as if they do not care what happens to their freedom.

That day, many of those around me chose not to think about the punishment until it was time to pay the debt and might not care to look back to the times that affected their future the most. For me, however, I found myself looking back to the most dangerous crossroads decisions that influenced the turns I took on the pathways that brought me back here again. That day, I would analyze each twisted turn I took and search for possibilities if I had taken another path at each of my fateful life-changing decisions.

Digging deeper into my past decisions, I saw people placed at the significant wrong turns my life took. Poor crossing guides were plentiful. I also saw people who stood ready to advise me of the better roads to follow. Evaluating my crossroad choices and the directions I listened to was how I would spend much of my time that day.

While I am not an expert on the criminal justice system, I qualify as an experienced veteran. I have yet to graduate from the school of hard knocks, but I have a long tenure in the academy of criminal behavior. I might argue none of us in this hall of worry feared the punishment enough to avoid the deeds that brought us to that judgment day.

What would have been the outcome of my life had I listened to the advice of those counseling me to steer clear of the wrong turns? Why was I so quick to push away the hands of good intentions and rush to follow the loudest and most foolish voices around me? Were the pleasures I experienced worth the struggles? That day, I would learn the answer. *Loud* and *unreasonable*, I now planned to be on guard against these enemies!

I was now aware how the unseen evil forces that stood ever-ready to push me deeper into life's miseries were also here that day. They were stepping out of the shadows to show their muscles in plain sight and boasting of their victories. The roar of their victory cries was deafening. That day, they had taken over the voices of many of my brothers and sisters throughout these halls of justice.

They boasted of their unlawful victories as if prison was a reward. With such a toxic environment, it is challenging to identify any Agents of Hope! In my first drug trafficking case in 1973, my dear Aunt Audrey Rector stood beside me, ready to intercede at that judgment time in my life. She was present and prepared to throw whatever help she could my way. She pleaded with the judge to give me a clean record after I completed my sentence. That day, she was no longer with me. No family stood beside me that day. I stood alone. Keeping us alone and without support was a goal of the enemy.

Aunt Audrey Rector

The finality of that day's proceedings caused some of us to be glad the justice system typically only slapped our hand and then released us through a revolving door. Sadly, those of us who feared the outcome of this day's verdicts appeared to be few. Could the boasting I heard be a tool the enemy uses to divert our attention away from a feeling of remorse? Diversion shows up often in our lives and was here today. No one around me that day was afraid of this enemy. Instead, they eagerly and blindly followed his lead without question.

Time To Think before Judgment

It was tough to think clearly in this courthouse that day. This waiting room filled to bursting with stories of destruction. Destruction sings a song of misery so well that the agents of loss and pain accompany him. Clarity is defeated, and confusion is the result.

Many of those pacing the halls that day would do a lot of worried waiting, myself included. Would my history qualify me as a habitual offender? At what point did the judge tire of seeing and forgiving the same offenses?

No seat would be comfortable, not that any of us would sit still for very long anyway. That day, some of us would seek comfort, but outstretched arms of condolence would be absent, replaced by emptiness. Impatience would also defeat peace. That day, the long hallways of this building would seem like continents, and time would creep slowly through the days of our past lives. Yes, that day was judgment day, and there would be painful thoughts of yesteryear. This place was not evil, but the influence of Evil was here.

During our time of pondering, a common thread ran among our fabric. The intangible feeling was that our past robbed us of our future. Was there an army of bad-luck soldiers sent to push us into poor choices and rob us of good fortune? We rarely considered this possibility as it was only a notion never quite surfacing into reality. Instead, we felt we were the cause of all of our mistakes. We each invited Evil into our decisions, but we did not realize he would work to completely own our lives and use us to promote even more of his evil plan once inside our being.

Some of those around me were telling their stories of yesteryear to anyone who would listen. Others quietly waited. Occasionally, I'd catch a familiar tale triggering memories of my troubled past. None of those around me were from my past, but a strange thread of familiarity ran throughout this room and down the halls. I was left with a distinct impression that although these people were all strangers to me, something familiar stood nearby and continued to influence our thoughts and decisions. Evil was nearby!

The supernatural captain of the enemy's army never showed his face or revealed his hand. This master of illusion dared not share his strategy to destroy our lives and keep us beaten down. Only the faint smell of decay was present. There was no physical evidence we could pin on him for our poor decisions. Still, each of us shared this ghost of a thought. Each of us now sensed something beyond our reach had controlled us on too many occasions.

Familiar Strangers around Me

Numerous strangers around me wore faces familiar to me. They reminded me of some of those who shared my troubled cross-roads. As I considered this familiarity, I realized most of the actual brothers and sisters who shared my rocky roads of despair were now gone, but despair was still here and was another soldier who had arrived to celebrate Evil's victories that day.

Some who shared my troubled roads were already in jail, some were dead, and some were like walking zombies because of years of substance abuse. While those allies of past miseries were not here that day, I felt a reserve army standing ready to replace their negative influence on our lives. We were never alone in our misery, and new soldiers were always waiting at the gates to our lives and ready to rush in.

Was there a secret file the judge would read that would tell more about our pasts than what was in that day's case files? Was there an evil influence that would coach the judge as he pondered our fates? Was it possible the commonality I felt was alive and traveled from person to person, leaving destruction in its path? These thoughts filled my head, and I was sure many more of us had the same suspicions.

If buildings could develop personalities, this one would wear a sad expression. We all agreed this was a horrible atmosphere! There were not enough rooms to hold us all while we waited our turn for judgment. Instead, we spent hours shuffling throughout a few confined spaces. No one looked content, and everyone looked nervous. Here and there, a few supporting family members gathered into groups, but mostly there were loners. I bet if we could look deeper into the shadows, there would be dark and evil images peering out and rejoicing in that day of reckoning, rejoicing in the pain of the moment. I got the distinct feeling a victory dance was happening all around us.

Contentment is the name of a mighty Angel of Peace. Contentment did not appear to be here that day. Nervous people, on the other hand, were in abundance!

My analysis of yesterday's poor choices I made saw many dark figures standing nearby, offering a push toward my destruction. I could put names on some of those hurtful helpers, while others always worked from the dark and were faceless, nameless influences. Many of those influences had been constant companions throughout my life. Some I foolishly chose to keep nearby. Others seemed to show up at the worst possible times in my life.

Curiously, not thinking about the results of following poor influences seemed to be typical for many of those present that day. Defiance provided a false sense of security here today. Defiance was among the loudest Opposing Agents and was rarely, if ever, subtle. He breeded a false sense of security that he used to his advantage.

For me, I tend to think constantly about the crossroads of my life. There were so many roads to take and so many choices to make. What if I had taken different routes or went another way? Yesterday, we had choices to make, and taking the wrong road felt right when we made that turn. Where were the traffic signs warning us of danger? Why couldn't we go back and change our direction?

Hope and Peace Seem Hard to Find Today

The feeling is that hope was not present in abundance here that day. Few felt hope was even possible. They had given up on hope.

All of us gathered together that day had walked the same winding roads. The twists and turns and the crossroads people we met along the way may have been different, but we all arrived at the same destination that day—judgment!

I was trying to clear my mind and think of healthy things. However, everywhere I looked and in every corner was something that reminded me of yesterday's trail of miseries. It was difficult to think clearly in this environment. I searched for peace, but I was distracted.

Instead of finding peace, there was an abundance of things that triggered memories of hurt. This fueled anger, and anger clouded good judgment! One negative emotion could start another, and I ended up confused.

Throughout the day, other reminders of tragic loss stepped into my view. Could an evil war general be standing nearby accompanied by the soldiers he used to bring about his plans of destruction on each of us? Were these reminders possible due to his desire to gloat over his victories and that he was nearby ready to claim even more victories? Yes, they were here. Evil influences were here! But

I had not given up on hope! It was vital to my survival to continue believing hope was possible.

Somehow, tiny bits of hope felt here stood firm and were not intimidated by all the evil soldiers around me. I wished there were more Agents of Hope.

Not all of the faces and influences along my journey were bad. As I searched through the crossroads of my travels, I saw numerous people who reached out with helping hands. Many of these guiding lights appeared often. While the faces of these souls who offered peace changed, the offerings of hope were constant. Also standing nearby was joy. Sadly, it was only that day I finally realized this.

With the losses of our pasts occupying our time that day, it was easy to stop believing in a happy future. Maybe this was the goal of our enemies. It was easy for my brothers of misery to embrace only the worst of our past crossroads and choose unrest over peace. One of these influences was loud and boisterous, and the other was always gentle. We decided to adopt rage, violence, and disrespect to survive in our world of Evil. These poisons were very effective at distracting us!

Focusing just on the people standing along my crossroads was not wise. Places also took on bad personalities or bad atmospheres. Some were easy to spot because of the volume they created. The same was true for the influences of people. Loud versus gentle. Was it possible noise could become a drowning influence against the Agents of Hope?

I have briefly met people who calmed my spirit with gentle words or smiles. Happiness had previously visited me, and I had hoped it would become a permanent friend of mine. I met those Angels of Hope many times but was not wise enough to recognize them until it was too late. I let something else drown out their influence.

Knowing that strangers have stepped into my crossroads and introduced me to their healthy joy has fueled my curiosity. I was convinced another unseen force was opposing the battle plan for my destruction. While I did not ask for this help, it continued to step into my crossroads without being invited.

Yes, there is hope for the hopeless, and it never gives up. I now knew my Aunt Audrey was such an Agent of Hope, and I was ready to explore others like her who desired to guide me, but was it too late? The evil liar would say yes, but hope rushed in with another answer. No, it was never too late!

Seeking out how I could better use these influencers of hope would occupy many of my future decisions. Seeking less obtrusive guidance would occupy more of my time in the future.

Well, they had finally called my first case to the courtroom, but something was different I hadn't yet mentioned. That day, I was on the *other* side. That day, I was the undercover police officer who made the drug buys that brought drug dealers to this courthouse of judgment. That day, I was paying some old dues!

How was this possible when I had such an extensive criminal history? I was a convicted drug dealer and a violent criminal, but that day, I had a clean record and had been free from drugs and alcohol since 1983. A significant reason for this are the Agents of Hope and peace like my Aunt Audrey and my Grandmother Blanche Stewart Lee, who paved the way with requests for intercession. As a police officer, it was not my desire to become an arresting agent of discipline. Instead, I chose to intervene at the crossroads of my brothers and sisters.

It is also imperative to mention that I serve a risen Savior. He defeated sin and death. His sacrifice makes my battle possible.

The battle plan analysis at the end of each chapter is a good resource for others to use. Making a list of the Evil versus the

Good we encounter makes it easier to spot *Trouble Traps* before they snare us!

I encourage you to keep such a list handy. Creating a list of the who, what, when, why, and how will reveal many places where the enemy dwells! Create a list and use it before making decisions. However, we must be honest when placing influences on one side or the other. Denial, distraction, confusion, and other Opposing Agents will work overtime to fool you into believing they support you. Being honest in your evaluation will be a very healthy step toward making good choices!

Battle Summary

This overview includes a summary of many people who were on trial on this date. I can't speak for each person's exact situation. However, in my fourteen years as a police officer, I learned enough to make some educated guesses about the evil influences each person experienced and had to live through.

I want to point out I often see more potential talent in these victims than in people who are generationally blessed or are not criminals! I suspect many of the *Trouble Traps* sent for these souls are because the Fallen Angels feared the positive impact they could have in their future. You can expect their future was attacked accordingly!

It is a fact that generationally cursed people are often *feared* by the Fallen One. Why? Because once saved, they can prove there is hope for even the most hopeless! They also know how to speak the language of pain and loss themselves.

My Home at the Miracle Hills Orphanage

I am very thankful for my time in the Miracle Hills Orphanage. This crossroads became my first remembered time of intercession. Going through the Miracle Hills orphanage door when I was age four or five is among my oldest memories. How and why I began the remembered years of my life in this place was once a concern. Now, I see it as another haven of hope that was at the crossroads of my life at precisely the time I needed one.

The first time I met lonely was just after I entered that building. Confusion and separation were also strangers to me who introduced themselves that day.

I genuinely believe my parents loved me, but I did not yet know the love of the type I would learn at Miracle Hills. That love came also came with peace. Today, I look back on my time in that orphanage as a blessing brought on through intercessory prayer. It came at just the right time in my life. I am thankful for what I learned there. Looking back, I can see healing hands in that place I did not know while I was there. The healing agent of good and others welcomed me in that place.

From my birth in 1953 until I entered Miracle Hills, I had lived continuously with my natural mother and father in upstate South Carolina, where then and now I have many blood relatives on both sides of my family living nearby. The bulk of my life has continued to be in this area. I was then and am now surrounded by family.

I can't recall the face of the person who took me through the front door at Miracle Hills and left me behind. I only remember the first day after I entered. At this early age, I did not know how to respond to the early morning struggle for clothes to wear for the day, and this often left me with no underwear and outer garments that would fit. Outside of this minor clothing issue, Miracle Hills was a blessing and came when I needed the life lessons I learned there.

Today, Miracle Hills has evolved into a beautiful haven of hope and peace for many. For me, it was added to a long list of miraculous intercessions in my life. That haven is forever embedded into my desires to point others to such havens of hope.

After a time at Miracle Hills, I eventually rejoined my mother and father. If I asked them why I spent time in the Miracle Hills Orphanage, I never got an answer from either of them. In later years, I asked this question of my other family members. The only answer I ever heard was that my mother was depressed. My father was not the source of this answer. I never heard a harsh word about my mother from him throughout his life, and he never talked about her depression or infidelity. Later, I would experience how her depression led her and me to many other bad places. Today in my professional role as a troubleshooter, I believe the cause of my mother's sinfulness was depression. The other Evils were the results.

The pain my father lived with and his silent reaction was a life lesson it took me far too long to learn. It ate at him on the inside, but on the outside, he continued to be strong for me, and I assume for my mother as well. The love he had for her must have been great!

Few harsh words were ever spoken to me about my mother by our family members. That speaks volumes about the strength of their character. What I knew of this Evil was by the experiences I lived while I was alongside her. My time at Miracle Hills must have been during the early days of her struggles with depression, as the Evils I write about were unknown to me before that time.

More specifically, before my time at Miracle Hills, I never knew Evil existed at all. Immediately following my time there was when I learned of Evil by experience.

I learned numerous valuable lessons at Miracle Hills that would impact my life for the rest of my years. I firmly believe our surroundings influence our life choices. This place provided a haven of hope. For a time, I had a defense against Evil at Miracle Hills.

Pain and healing battled over me at Miracle Hills. One fun day at Miracle Hills, I sat on the hood of a farm tractor for a ride. I made the mistake of grabbing the exhaust pipe with both hands and received severe burns as a result. I had now learned two new emotions of which I had no prior experience. Struggle and pain had both harshly introduced themselves to me, and I had not prepared for either of their arrivals.

At Miracle Hills, I also learned that struggle and pain would not be present in a place they promoted, a place they called heaven. What an exciting thought! I had not heard of that place before. They also talked of a healer named Jesus. I was curious!

My mother and father never talked of such things, but I would later learn they both knew of and believed in Jesus. However, for me, this was a new concept. I learned enough about Jesus during my time there to respect him. The seed was well sown in me, and I thank Miracle Hills for it.

Many of my earliest memories centered around things I loved and things I hated or feared. Emotions in the middle rarely came my way. That day on the tractor, pain came to visit, and he set up residence alongside his ally named struggle, and both intended to list my life as their permanent address. Yes, they both embedded themselves into my memories at a very early age. I remember them both, but not because of my love for either of them.

That day, I would not be left to learn how to deal with pain and struggle by myself. After the staff gave me immediate first aid, a young girl came to comfort me. She spent considerable time relaxing me and bringing me peace. She, too, was away from her parents. Or was she? Could this girl have been a Heavenly Agent of comfort sent to combat the Opposing Agents' intent on my misery and ultimate destruction? I have often wondered about this. Comfort and peace battled with pain and struggle for me that day, and an angel of mercy was my life coach.

Who was this girl who brought me comfort, and how did her life turn out? I expect she brought comfort and peace to others throughout her days. She instilled in me the desire to do the same. This earthly (or heavenly) angel proved to me we could impact the lives of others and should be on the lookout for times to assist those we encounter in the crossroads of our life's journey.

The result of this angel caring for me became a remembered and lifelong lesson. For a time, the peace she shared with me lasted. Eventually, her mercy was forgotten and replaced with rage. Then one day, something triggered my memory of the lessons she taught me.

At such a young age, is it possible we can learn healthy lifelong lessons? Oh yes! We may push them away, but love never dies, and mercy never dies. They are both eternal!

I also learned fear during those days but not how to handle it wisely. During a lunch period, two older boys began to fight. I had never experienced fighting around me. If my parents fought, I don't remember it. My reaction to this fight was to run out of the building and into a safe hiding place. This early angel of mine found my hiding place. She came to my rescue again. I wonder if a search of the records at Miracle Hills would reveal her name?

Today, I am aware of the fact that angels do walk among us, and they occasionally appear in human form when a life-changing healing is needed or a life lesson is a goal. Was she earthly or heavenly? Whichever she may have been, her influence accompanies me today. Later, other angels would arrive to intercede for me just before I was to make major mistakes.

After this fight, the adult leaders offered words to comfort me. They were not successful. My way of dealing with fear would soon become violence. I became capable of being violent. At this crossroads of my life, the battle to harm me through fear won a victory. Fear came to live alongside struggle and pain.

Did this new Evil named violence sleep until my third-grade year? Soon after that day, when violence reappeared, death came to take my mother. Looking back on my past, I have seen other times when Evil visited just before a major battle against me.

My oldest memory of spiritual warfare in my life was during my time at Miracle Hills. The army of Evil grew, but peace was still nearby, silently building the walls to my fortress.

All military war plans see phases—first, an initial attack, then others. You can count on them to include diversions, deceptions, and divisions. You can also count on them to hide the real targets. The same is true for attacks from Evil. First, a little pain, then fears, and soon depression or loneliness follows. Before long, our lives become victims of a variety of attacks we never saw coming. One misery invites another, and sadly our reactions can add fuel to this plan for our final destruction.

Maybe the most harmful experience I learned during those days was loneliness. Struggles and pains are often short-term experiences, but once fear and loneliness begin their work against us, their efforts are constant. We can resolve struggles, and pain can subside, but the Evil named fear and his brother loneliness are harder to handle. Both can and intend to be permanent influencers.

My story is not one of total loss. No, instead, it ends as a story of significant victories. There are ways to counter each of these enemies.

From the days at Miracle Hills and throughout my life, such battles have raged against me, but I have been rescued countless times by angels like this young girl and many earthly souls with similar hearts. There have also been miraculous rescues that could only have come from supernatural forces. They had to have come from heavenly intercession. They came to me before I believed in them, heaven, or Jesus.

Know this: I am not unique. Mercy is also within reach for you—always!

As you begin to seek peace, your memories will return to times when Heavenly Angels interceded at your crossroads. You will also learn of times when they acted on your behalf, with the result being you missed a planned attack against yourself. These intercessions are harder to spot. I challenge you to spend some quiet time seeking the "what ifs" of such times. Had I taken more of the wrong turns at the crossroads of my life, far more of the agents of misery would have won victory over me. Rescue is always nearby but rarely recognized when Evil is making so much noise.

At each of these crossroads, the people and resources used to deliver me out of harm's way are stories of victory. Each of us finds ourselves at crossroads outside of our ability to negotiate wisely without guidance, but good crossroads guides of earthly and heavenly types are within your reach. How to spot those helping hands and recognize unhealthy directions is hard, especially in real-time. For far too long, I learned to spot them only by looking back on my mistakes. That's not the smart way to learn. Good decisions can be made in real-time with some practice by recognizing and resisting the evil hands that reach out to us and call themselves our friends.

Learning how to deal with troubles is a lesson I often learned by making the wrong choices. I did not see the hands of the helpful crossing guards. So, I lost many battles. Today, a study of my mistakes and how victory came my way is well worth the time! It will teach you how to do the same.

Note that finding a helpful guide may require some discipline in both looking for and listening to them. Also note that while reviewing my false turns, I could spot helpers standing ready to guide me on the correct path. This practice took some study, but it is worth the effort!

I must also share that some of our mistakes will take several steps to counter, which means you can't always see an instant recovery from a battle. Stay the course! Patience is the name of an angel of hope! And don't let loneliness convince you that you are alone. Make a few steps toward healthier places and people.

After the death of my mother, loneliness became a significant and early burden for me, but very soon, I would again encounter the Evil named death, who also had my name on his hit list at an early age! His plan also included making loneliness grow in my life.

Do Angels Exist?

arrived at the answer to this question through studying the events of my past life. Long before I believed in Jesus or angels, I had met Evil face to face and did not like it. I knew something existed that felt wrong. Being surrounded by unnatural things I grew to accept as a regular part of my life during my earliest days slowed my learning. What felt wrong took years to see as Evil, and it took the intervention of both heavenly and earthly influences to teach me how to identify good from bad.

What I had grown to accept as usual or normal was not. My time at Miracle Hills was the place where I began to see another side of life. I felt something new there. It was the fact angels protected that place and were busy growing peace, hope, and joy. However, before I could use this knowledge to help me fight battles against Evil, more damage was ahead. While we cannot call upon angels on demand, a lot can be learned by studying how they operate in our lives.

Do I have proof? I think so. How the existence of angels and intercession can change lives came to me through analyzing my own life's experiences. It was not through any Bible study or church attendance, which would come later. Jesus Christ was very new to me, and I did not know him at all. But he knew me!

I saw so many rescues in my past I had to admit something was at work, but faith is the correct doorway, and the proof is not. See Romans 10:17 and Hebrews 11:1, 6.

After searching the crossroads of my life and knowing Jesus as my Lord, I often spotted intercession, the extent of which was overwhelming! I eventually realized only Jesus Christ himself could have sent both human intercessors and Heavenly Angels to my numerous rescues.

Some peace had come before I accepted him as my Savior. However, true joy and a much more profound peace had not. I knew of Jesus and his work long before I believed in him as my Savior. Don't count on becoming a child of the risen King Jesus by finding proof first!

The written words of God are his Bible. This book starts with a vital lesson about using trust and not proof. Let me explain. To start, let me share I am not concerned about time. Time only exists for our benefit. It does not exist outside of our lives. There are no thoughts of time in eternity. When events happen and how long they take is not something we can even comprehend. For far too long, I tried to fit the stories in the Bible into a timeline.

None of us are pre-determined to die and go to hell. How the creator God works this out is not something I am an expert on. What I do know is that no matter our past, we can be forgiven and enter heaven if we accept Christ as our Lord and ask for our sins to be forgiven.

I will tell you of fantastic rescue attempts sent my way while I was not a believer. That brings up a question about how and why I was rescued if I was not a Christian. There are several things to consider to arrive at an answer:

1. Christ knew I would one day ask him if I could use my story to reach others who, like me, have lived a horrible life and have given up on hope. Since time only exists on this earth, he could rescue me before I ever asked to use my story to reach others. He knew one day I would have this desire.

2. Through generational blessings asked for by my ancestors, he desired to send intercession to honor their prayers of righteousness.
3. Through earthly loved ones praying for my future, he sent intercession.

One day, when I see Jesus, I will immediately know more of the whys but won't care about the hows! Here is a vital lesson for those who have ears to listen:

At the dawn of creation, Adam and Eve needed nothing (Gen. 1:29, 2:8–25). There was a peace that evolved around their trust in the creator God. When the Fallen One, Satan, appeared to them, he tempted them to think another way. That thought was to eat the fruit of the tree of the knowledge of Good and Evil (Gen. 3:1–6).

Up until his visit, they trusted and had total faith in God. Satan tempted them to question God and look for other answers. They ate the fruit that caused them to question their trust in God about feeding them. Faith and trust fell victim that day.

This one lie introduced a major sin into our future. The evil one himself made his mark on our lives with this first Evil, a lie! Now we seek proof before having faith.

Since 1995, I have been a consultant in the electronics technology of smart homes and low voltage systems used in commercial manufacturing. Often, I must find the causes of electronic failures. I use logical approaches for solving problems. We all do, and there are times when we should use this process. Analyzing, researching, and finding proof has and will continue to improve the human race.

It is not, however, the way to eternal peace. Instead, trust is the correct doorway. After adopting this act of faith, proof abounds. As I said earlier, I learned of Evil's existence, which made me search for evidence about good and bad, true and false, existing at all. The search for evidence was the wrong method to use. I did see evidence in my life regarding outside forces at work. Curiosity opened my eyes. Heavenly and Earthly Angels were everywhere after that. Once I had trusted, faith followed and then proof was everywhere.

Be very careful with these words. If you go on a hunt for evidence before trusting Jesus, you are destined to fail. Evidence is the opposite of faith. Before I was saved, I saw the face of Evil. I write to illustrate Evil, not to offer it as a way to eternal peace. During my time in the USAF, I met faith and was saved. The hunt for evidence *was not* the resource used! Many rescues came my way before my day of salvation.

Of course, I abbreviate this story. Understanding the events of my life must include trust before proof. The book of Genesis starts with a prefix that shares how to get off to a good start. It emphasizes how trust is essential for understanding. It also warns about lies from the very beginning.

Today, I am years into the discipline of a daily study of God's Word and worshipful attendance in his house. Now, I see much more clearly. I see proof everywhere!

While most of the intercessions on my behalf came through humans acting like Earthly Angels, I have also seen Heavenly Angels in human form (Heb. 13:2). Sadly, I did not realize this until after my rescue(s). Throughout each of our lives, we come into contact with Heavenly Angels in human form. Spotting them in real-time is very rare, if not impossible.

Before we move ahead, let me describe the differences in angels.

Heavenly Angels are from eternal heaven. They act unseen most often but do occasionally appear in human form.

- Hebrews 12:22
- Psalm 68:17

- Daniel 10:12–13
- Jude 1:9

Intercessors are humans who pray for our intercession. Some may not even know those who they pray over. Some of our ancestors also prayed for intercession for all their generations to follow. Intercessors also pray for the community and world.

- Psalm 16:3
- Romans 1:7
- Revelation 14:12

Earthly Angels are humans volunteering to be used as agents of peace, love, hope, and a wide variety of other good things. They also stand ready as our life coaches and crossing guards. I met many of these. Some I followed, and it changed my life in positive ways.

Life Coaches: Best Friend Ted Hrizak,
Greer High Nurse Nellie Gordon
Greer SC Police Chief Dean Crisp

Fallen Angels are those who chose to follow Satan as he rebelled against God. Their punishment was their exile to earth, and they are among us. He and they are the source of the Evil we encounter.

- Isaiah 14:12–14
- Jude 1:6
- 2 Peter 2:4

My Home in Rio De Janeiro, Brazil

S ometime after my home at Miracle Hills, my parents came for me, and I rejoined them. I carried with me some expectations I never had before. Among them was the desire to be held, comforted, and protected from fear. Sadly, the comfort I experienced at Miracle Hills did not travel with me when I left that haven. Fear did travel with me and grew in strength.

There was a time after I learned about true and healthy love when I resented not being held by my mother or father. This feeling was a victory against me and robbed me of peace and, more importantly, learning forgiveness. After I learned the power of forgiving others, I began to remember times I was held and comforted by my parents.

The lesson to learn is how some feelings (lack of forgiveness) can blind our judgment.

Before I can share success stories, I must share the losses I encountered and the miracles. This chapter illustrates one of my earliest miraculous rescues.

After my time in the Miracle Hills Orphanage, many negative things were coming at my family all at once. Death came for me when we moved to Brazil, but he was not the only enemy that attacked us there.

It became hard to identify the most harmful influences of all the things I spotted in our past. Today, I can see how depression was the most damaging enemy for my mother. Distractions, diversions, and confusion worked to keep us from realizing the depth of his danger.

At age five, I boarded a plane with my mother, and together we flew to Rio De Janeiro, Brazil, to join my father. Depression traveled with us.

I remember sitting in my mother's lap several times on that trip. From this, I know comfort was present. However, comfort was under attack, and its positive influence on my life was significantly reduced. I do not remember ever sitting in Mother's lap again after that airplane ride.

Why we traveled to Rio was a mystery to me for years. At first thought, it was only because my father was a talented repairman of looms used in cotton mills. It may also have been to help my mother get past her depression. However, this move opened the door for new miseries to enter her life, and her depression only grew.

Becoming depressed over mistakes is common and may seem innocent in the beginning. For my mother and many others, depression grew no matter where she traveled. This enemy of our well-being is a living and evil force working to destroy those it infects. Its plan to destroy us also followed us to Rio.

Rio was possible because my father was a "fixer." With only a sixth-grade education, he became so skilled as a mechanic in the textile industry that his "loom fixer" skills would open many doors. His approach to solving problems was contagious and influenced my children, Anthony and Melanie, their children, and myself. This is an example of generational blessings.

In my profession as a smart house consultant, I use a fixer approach to every trouble call. To succeed, you must focus more on the cause than on the symptoms. It is easy to focus more on the pain than on what is causing it. This distraction is a stealth master. Knowing this is vital to analyzing problems. Moving thousands of miles away from the cause of my mother's depression changed the scenery but did not approach the reason. Dad missed that diagnosis.

I learned electronics in a USAF classroom, but I learned how to "fix" by the "burn and learn" method. Today, I know where solutions are because I recovered from the pain of making hurtful mistakes. Learning not to touch a hot stove should not be discovered after the pain of feeling it! "Burn and learn" is absolutely the wrong way to learn.

The Evil of distraction works hard to keep us avoiding pain before it happens. It loves the "burn and learn" method and, more importantly, most often succeeds in its goal of diverting our attention to the symptoms rather than the causes of our troubles.

It is easy to go through our lives thinking no factors outside our actions can impact our future. The evil enemy of loneliness fuels this erroneous thought. Miracles and great intercession were fighting unseen battles for my family and me.

Knowing this begins the journey to peace and works on the causes of our troubles.

One day in Rio, death came for me but was defeated, although it was years before I even knew death called for me at all. The intercession sent my way that day was not private. It is available to you. Start looking for causes and stop focusing on pain, and your vision will get better!

Our home in Rio was in an apartment building that overlooked Copacabana Beach. We only had to walk across the street to enjoy this fantastic beach. In Rio, Copacabana Beach joins another beautiful beach known as Ipanema Beach. There is a rock wall that juts out into the ocean, separating the two coasts. The place where these two beaches intersect would become where my earliest remembered delivery from death occurred.

Death is the final agent we will all meet one day. I really can't decide if death is an agent of Good or Evil. Maybe both? Either way, death visited and almost claimed me that day.

It began as a typical day where we planned to spend the day enjoying the beach. During my early years, I was full of excess energy. This may explain how I got away from my family and into the ocean. I entered the water right at the rock wall separating Copacabana Beach from Ipanema Beach.

2004, The exact place in Rio, where the current took me underwater in 1959 and slammed me hard into that rock wall.

While entirely underwater, I was being pushed by the current into those rocks. Still underwater and injured, I was headed out to sea and certain death, but my journey to death ended when my underwater body suddenly wrapped around the feet of an adult swimming further out into the ocean. He reached down and pulled me up and out of the water.

I was beaten and bruised, but I was saved from certain death by a man who never saw me until he pulled me from around his legs and above the water.

Who was this man? It was my father! But he didn't even know I was in the water. I find it no coincidence my rescue came at the feet of my earthly father and was also at the will of my heavenly Father!

This miracle was among the first of a long string of incredible, impossible miracles that would come my way. Over the years to come, many other rescuers would join the list of those who would provide miraculous intercessions for me. Some of them were Heavenly Angels who took the form of humans for my rescue. Some were earthly humans who volunteered to fight battles for me.

Who was to blame for me entering the water unsupervised? Was it my mother who lost track of me that day? Or was it an agent of extra energy called hyperactivity? Who left me unsupervised was not the real cause of my near-death experience, but on that day, it was most likely the topic of discussion. Today, I see another hidden reason. The Fallen One knew silent prayer warriors were asking for intercession for my future. So, he knew I might one day positively impact others if I lived. Satan is not omniscient like God. Instead, he must react to what he sees. For far too long, I was easy to predict.

Maybe this one rescue mission made Satan realize my future could help others find rescue's source. Diversion masked this battle plan for my life, turning it into a hunt for those who did not supervise me that day. The Evil named distraction helped hide the real battle plan.

Fixers spend time analyzing the most likely cause of an event, and we often stop our search when we decide what or who is the most likely cause. Fixers like me can become so over-confident in our diagnosis that we can miss the real reason. The enemies of my future named pride and over-confidence had their way with me for years. Their victories blinded my ability to see, but my blindness was not permanent.

We all missed the real cause of my near-death experience that day. If the Opposing Agent of confusion is present, you, too, will most likely be diverted away from seeing the truth, and its symptoms will hide the cause. Remember this: The first Evil humankind saw was when Satan lied to Eve. See Genesis 3:1–5.

My near-death experience was indeed a life-changing event and almost a life-ending event. Lack of supervision put me in that water, but once I was in, something outside of inadequate care grabbed me and pushed me toward my death. Was this simply bad luck? I don't believe in luck very much. Fixers search for the cause, and luck is rarely a factor in our hunt.

There was also another unseen force that countered Evil's actions, pushing me out to sea. This force led my father to be in the water at the right place and moment. Subtle and seemingly unrelated events must also be analyzed, especially in life-altering events and decisions.

That day at age five, a plan existed to end my life. Does such a plan still exist today? Yes! This plan will undoubtedly intensify after this book is published. The search for why has made me more alert. It has also helped me to avoid going into troubled waters since then. Sadly, It would take far too many near-death experiences for me to finally learn to avoid eagerly rushing into dangerous waters again.

There would be many other times similar miracles would happen in my life, many of which could only have come from the impact of the unseen forces of our Lord Jesus, but during many of my most troubled years, I did not believe Heavenly Angels existed at all. Worse yet, I did not think Evil existed either. However, I was to become known as Evil Me before I learned the truth.

While unseen forces impact all of our lives, the choices we make and actions of other people around us account for the vast majority of our life-altering paths. Guard the pathways into your life to avoid inviting Evil inside. Once inside, Evil will invite other soldiers to attack. Misery *does* like company.

This event on Copacabana Beach taught me some life-saving lessons. Years later, I realized there was a healthy path to take at each of my crossroads and a dangerous one. Looking back in time is not the smart way to plan for tomorrow. Looking in my rear-view mirror tended to emphasize my bad choices more than the good ones.

It was much easier to see the wrong turns because they were the ones quickly leading to some form of destruction or pain. Searching the crossroads of my past, I began to notice which factors influenced me to make each turn. Often, a person was influencing me on the first few turns away from a happy destination. Today, I can see the harm that came from following the guidance of such influences. I can also see the faces of the more gentle crossing guards who stood ready to point me in the right direction. Many of these I resented or ignored. Some I even hurt. Some gave up on reaching out to me, and others did not.

We lived in Rio for a couple of years, and I remember many happy times. Since my mother never worked, we spent a lot of time together on the beach and seeing the fantastic sites nearby. I have many fond memories of our time together there.

Of all my childhood memories, Rio was the happiest of times when I was with my mother. Dad's older brother and his family joined us for a time in Rio. My older cousins then added to the joy of our time in Rio, during which we built an unbreakable bond that continues to this day. Their mother, Hazel Jones Stewart, would also later take on a much-needed role as a crossroads guide for me. For years into the future, she had me in her heart and never lost track of where I was and what I was doing. She and other mentors like her never gave up on me. Aunt Hazel would become one of my early Earthly Angels who would silently intercede for me.

Aunt Hazel was one of the few people who praised me when I was right and stood firmly against me when I was wrong. It would be far too many years later when I would realize the value of such guidance and even longer before adopting the strength of character she, her children, and grandchildren embody. Always appreciate those like Aunt Hazel who choose to intercede for you. Also, do not push anyone away who opposes your mistakes.

Today, it is much easier to see how good intentions grow healthy relationships. I took for granted the peace that came from being with my mother while we were in Rio. How peace and joy came each day was not a concern. For those two years in Rio, I did not have to work to find a happy place.

There is a migration leading to happiness. It starts with who we surround ourselves with and is heavily impacted by what we do together. When we left Rio a couple of years later, peace and joy stayed behind. The evil agent of death went with us instead. He would soon visit again, and this time he would have a victory—or so he thought!

Can Places Fuel Evil?

C an places fertilize Evil? Yes! This fertilization begins with the character of people who visit or live there. The Word of God tells us principalities do have angels assigned to them. Assignments are also given to angels to guard each of us well ahead of our birth. My guardian angels have been busy! See Acts 8:26, Hebrews 1:14, and Hebrews 13:2.

If we frequent a place that fuels our bad habits and addictions, we should expect Evil to be there. The angels assigned to guard us may have to face enormous enemies based on our choices of places to visit. Be careful with distractions in areas you frequent. It should be easy to spot peace. If any influence drowns out peace, then expect to lose your ability to spot Evil easily.

Both Heavenly and Fallen Angels are assigned to places, governments, and principalities. See Daniel 10:13. We must learn to spot the areas where the enemy controls the atmosphere and avoid such sites. Mother never knew this. Places she visited opened the door for the final enemy named heroin to enter her life. It was in Rio where she began to take me with her into these places.

Also, note that Evil loves to gloat. Careful observation often spots Evil nearby. Before indulging in the busyness of noise or lights, invest a little time into searching the shadows. You will also spot people under the influence of Evil who parade themselves and their choices out in the open. Occasionally, you may also spot the handprint of Evil itself.

Many of the most infected places of Evil have an attraction, one that draws in its prey like a moth to a flame. Somewhere in Rio, my mother fell victim to such an attraction and subsequently made some horrible decisions. This trap is hard to spot before it becomes dangerous. This trap also rarely lets go of its prey. The Fallen Angel over such evil principalities is a strong warrior!

Depression is hard to fight. Instead, my mother chose a new companion to drown her depression. That companion was heroin and was found in a place she decided to visit. This powerful seducer was hiding somewhere near my mother in Rio in the 1950s. It lured her inside, and then it followed her back to the United States. While in Rio, she most likely only had to take a few steps away from peace to this destination of misery.

Accompanying my mother into that place were indeed the demons named depression, loneliness, and addiction. They walked with my mother into this place, and she never spotted them until it was too late. She pushed her angel(s) of hope to the side and embraced misery instead. She placed me on top of the bar to dance for the crowd. The crowd applauded. Evil smiled in a dark corner somewhere nearby.

Later, as a young adult, the curse of visiting the wrong places followed me and grew in strength. The point to consider is how a seemingly innocent event in our past can return with the intent to harm us years later. Evil comes in many forms and lies in waiting. I have not danced on a bar top in many years and never will again.

Years later, I traveled back to Rio with my wife and son. There are many beautiful things I can say about this city, but there are also places where Evil grows and lies in wait, and not just in Rio. During my second visit, some fantastic and healthy things happened in Brazil. On this trip, we joined our Mount Lebanon church group in Fortaleza, Brazil, to build a new wing onto the Davis Lar Orphanage.

Anthony Stewart with children from the Davis Lar Orphanage in 2004.

This place had a hedge of angels guarding its gates!

Once again, the turns of my life included an orphanage! Today, I would not hesitate to travel back to Rio. I would, however, be on guard as to the places I visit while I am there. This lesson applies to every future destination we choose to visit. Watch the shadows for Evil gloating and claiming his prize too early.

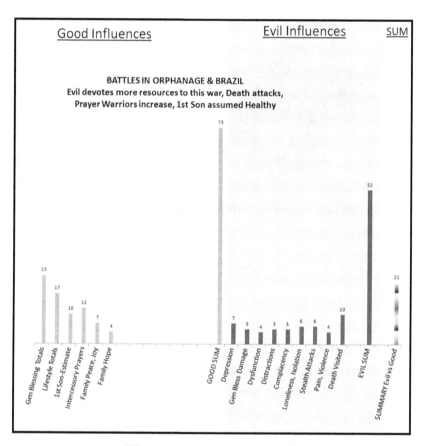

The plan to destroy ramps up!

I Learn of an Unknown Brother

Until our return to the USA from Brazil, I thought we were a family of three. I was wrong.

My family of three and an old companion named depression returned to the USA. Depression was familiar, but now it had grown in strength. The damage it intended to inflict would soon prove deadly. Its attack plan centered around the fact that my mother had another son five years before me. Depression used separation from this son to dominate my mother.

Not including the supernatural enemy named depression, our family should have totaled four. It would be many years later before I learned of this brother. Mother, however, had suffered over this daily.

Dad returned to his career as a fixer in upstate South Carolina in the textile industry, and I entered the first grade. Looking back, we bordered on being poor, but I never knew it. I give a lot of credit to my father for this feeling, and I never remember being hungry or cold, at least not while in my own home. Dad made this possible by working two shifts much of the time. Mom never worked, which proved to be a mistake. She had too much time on her hands.

Our family was once again together in the area where so many other members of both sides of our family lived, but something was different. Something sinister had traveled with us on our return to the USA. Depression accompanied us and brought with it addiction. These enemies attacked my mother fiercely when we returned to the USA and lasted until I was nine years old when they took her life. After her death, addiction soon struck me and won a significant victory. Depression, however, never gained a stable foothold in my life as it had in my mother's, but its Evil rubbed off on me through her acts.

It would be many years after my mother's death before I would learn of the cause of her depression. While she was alive, we lived with the symptoms.

There is a way to restore joy and peace in the most damaged of lives, and there is a way to cast out the evil demon known as depression and his accompanying brother, addiction. In my mother's case, she could never turn loose of the cause of her depression. Instead, she let the symptoms ruin her life.

Fixing the cause of a problem is difficult when we choose to dwell on past mistakes. Stressing over things we can't change is a recipe for recurring misery and an invitation to pending disasters. Not letting the symptoms of our past mistakes defeat us is mandatory for healing.

By now, you can see how Evil often sneaks in. He looks for a small crack and slides into our being. Depression is often not the first doorway he uses.

It would be best to also realize how Evil often invites his allies to join him in a predictable order. For example, mistakes in relationships can bring in hurt to take up residence, who then invites loneliness, who then invites depression, who invites drugs and alcohol. I know of no formula to share with you. Instead, I ask you to evaluate each uninvited and invisible stranger who enters your life. You should also be alert to how these battles come in phases, just like they do during world wars.

In addition, If any battle commander can keep his war plans secret, he is sure to win. I have learned this the hard way. However, Opposing Agents can't permanently hide their character. Depression, loneliness, and violence are just a few of the names of the evil soldiers sent against us. While we can't see their entire battle plan or predict its exact order, we can quickly know the enemies by their names and character. Depression is evil! Mother never understood this. I learned of its evil before it killed me like it did my mother in 1963.

How I learned of the cause of her depression was another life-changing event. It happened many years later, while I was working with my passion for genealogy and publishing a history of my mother's family, the Gambrells.

I called, requesting some information from Uncle Kenneth Gambrell, a younger brother to my mother. I did not expect to hear him asking me to include my brother in the genealogy book I planned to publish.

Until that day, I did not know I had a brother. I learned from Uncle Kenneth my mother had a son five years before I was born while she was quite young and unmarried. She gave him up for adoption. His adoption was through some very close relations.

He was so close to our family that my mother saw and could visit him often. She was able to visit him from the time he was a newborn. This closeness grew into depression. After I was born, she saw him less often. Today, I am not sure who or where my brother is or how he is doing.

Mother never told him who he was or that she was his mother. Maybe this was the reason we lived in Brazil for a couple of years. It was a way to give her a chance to heal. If so, it did not work. Depression grew while she could not visit him. Was this the leading cause of her sorrow? Maybe, but I will never know for sure.

How did she lose him? Why was he not my brother while she was alive? At my brother's birth, she lived with an older sister, her sister's husband, and their mother. She was making lifestyle mistakes that could not have been approved by her supporting family members. So, a bargain to allow the adoption and never tell my brother the truth began.

It is crucial at this point to state that the Gambrell family was not generationally cursed. They were instead generationally blessed.

Front Kenneth, LuVadie, Annette,
Back Row, Joe, Jack, Ralph, Venice, Faye, Mother (Betty)

Her mistakes began her depression, and being so close to a son she loved so dearly and could visit fueled her depression. My mother certainly made mistakes, major mistakes, but I am finally at peace with her. Sadly, she could never find peace herself. With no peace, joy also never arrives. The journey to total misery grows with the arrival of each new enemy.

Misery has a tendency and desire to become contagious. That contagion reached out to both my father, myself, and possibly my brother.

Our extended families made a point never to discuss any mistakes my mother had made. That left me to make some educated guesses. My fixer personality is never satisfied with guessing! So, I continued to play out the details of my mother's past and looked for signs I could explore.

The end goal was to identify the "cause" of her depression and eliminate it in my life and the lives of my family before it could take root in their lives.

While we can't always fix or avoid every pothole in the road, this search for the cause of my mother's depression did teach me to be alert to signs that often appear before we encounter life's other *Trouble Traps*. The complete step-by-step battle plans against us are rarely predictable and use seemingly random logic. However, the character of the evil influences can be spotted before the most damage is done.

Yes, I still lose battles, and yes, I still make mistakes! The enemy named Evil will always win some of the battles planned against us, but recovering from lost skirmishes is now quicker and often awards a major trophy called peace!

With a bit of training, looking for and spotting signs of Evil gets easier. On the beach that day in Rio, there was such a sign that came right before I entered the water. The Fallen One gloated over my death a little too soon.

I specifically remember a colossal manta ray jumping entirely out of the water. Everyone on the beach gasped at this sight. Maybe that was also sent to distract my mother? Was this also a sign from the evil one that he had arrived? At first consideration, this event may seem to be unrelated, but as I studied other crossroads experiences I encountered later in life, I often noticed similar signs just before Evil arrived. Evil loves to gloat and often does so prematurely.

Sin can be so arrogant as to prematurely boast over its pending victory. I have seen such signs too many times to write this off as a coincidence. At the very least, I have learned to watch for such signs of danger! This simple skill has often saved me and those around me.

The critical point is how noisy and busy places make it hard to spot these warning signs. Do this: The next time you are in a busy place filled with distractions, take some time to search. Watch the people around you. Chances are you will spot some unusual things. Do this each time you enter such places, and you may see Evil nearby.

Yes, places can breed evil! Or, at the very least, create an environment where Evil feels no need to hide.

I now believe our surroundings and choice of who we associate with often fuels miseries. It is equally vital we learn to grasp the hands of the often unlikely people around us who offer guidance against Evil.

It is also imperative to discuss how our decisions always begin a journey. Even the simplest of choices start a series of events. For example, depression opened the door to my mother's addiction, which led to her death when I was nine years old, right at a time in my life when I needed her the most. This event falsely made me think I was to follow in the footsteps she took. Yes, we can be a product of our environment, good or bad.

Only noting the beginning and end of a journey is a critical mistake. There are always twists and turns in the middle. There is a plan to rob us all of peace and joy. I can illustrate how there is always a way back to peace in the middle of the wrong course. Mother only saw the beginning of her misery. She fell for the lie there could never be a happy future without my brother. She gave up too early.

With the claws of depression so deeply embedded into my mother, what could she expect to come next? What came next is a guess, but it is probably a good guess that depression needed help to obliterate her. Mother had a strong support group nearby while we were in upstate South Carolina. Her local family and my father's family included many who could show her the right roads to follow. Our time in Rio removed us from them. Spending two years away from our support group of family members proved not to be the best plan. The trip to Rio removed us from a healthy support group, and separation became the name of a new enemy.

Could it be that depression invited separation, who then invited heroin to attack my mother? I strongly suggest we all slow down and question each bad thing we encounter to see if we can predict and then avoid the next agent of misery who will arrive!

Can places breed Evil? What do you think?

Mother and me just before we flew to Rio in 1958
and before depression overtook her.

Depression had a human ally in the battle plan to destroy her. At this point in her journey, it is essential to note how this battle plan also meant certain destruction for my father and me.

What was the name of heroin's ally in Rio? Was it a friend? Could it have been a trusted friend who coaxed her into trying heroin? Did this introduction happen inside a bar? Somebody introduced her to this Evil. This Evil was very contagious. Whoever it was, this "friend" was next in the list of *Trouble Traps* on her journey to death and my journey to a life of misery and pain.

Soon, my father's use of alcohol dug in with its claws of destruction. Misery loves company and is very contagious! Was I to be the next victim of these evil soldiers? Was this fact predictable?

For my mother, depression was the start, and drugs were the end. Heroin was the final stop on her road to a destination named death. Had she gotten off the train just before heroin entered her life, she might have found her way back to start over, but drugs bring with them many distractions. Now the journey to death was rolling faster down the track. At each stop along the route, many other passengers of Evil boarded the train.

Good decisions require clearness of thought. Distractions fight against clarity! Without the clearness of thinking (that comes with peace), it is easy to get diverted to the wrong destination. We must know the train we travel on through life can always arrive at the wrong destination. Whatever we planned for our life, wherever my mother hoped to go in life, now seemed impossible to her. Heroin bought the ticket for the destination known as death. Mom purchased the heroin, but a trusted friend most likely opened the door.

Depression digs in deeper just before the final destination and convinces us how hopeless our life is and can make us forget through his friend named addiction! Once we find ourselves at the wrong place and believe all hope is lost, giving in to death comes next. With so many missteps in our life's plan, we can't even find the way back to the station for a ride to a happier place. Our joy became lost long ago, so we find temporary relief in the addictions available to us. I understand this because addictions also ruled my life for a time.

With heroin being so plentiful to her in Rio, her life would end quicker. With our return to the USA, she added alcohol to her list of addictions. She also found suppliers for her heroin addiction and probably any other drug of opportunity. She took me with her on these journeys to bad places where forgetfulness could replace depression. Upon my return to the USA when I was seven years old, my happy childhood ended. Her enemies covertly attacked me before we traveled to Brazil, and when we returned, they no longer hid their intentions. Destruction joined forces with them with a war plan against her, my father, and me.

And yes, she sat me on top of more bars to dance. The crowd applauded and gave me the money Mother spent on drugs and alcohol.

The plan of death and destruction to stop future generations exists before we are born. How is this possible? It is because our past ancestors asked for their future generations to be protected and blessed. So the Fallen Angel Satan planned to fight those generational blessings.

Today, my children and grandchildren are all touching the lives of others in powerful ways. The Evil named death had a plan to stop them before they were born, but a more powerful force has the opposite strategy.

Know this: generational blessings are under attack! As each new generation arrives, the number of people asking for protection for the next generation is shrinking. Ending generational blessings is a goal of the enemy!

Distance is a close companion of separation and can take on multiple different faces. It is certainly wise to know when to be distant from Evil. However, my mother's most potent enemy named depression traveled with us everywhere we went. We became comfortable with that lifestyle.

My mother intended to hide many of her actions from my father. This plan failed, but it did succeed at making him distant. His workaholic attitude became his way to escape misery. It also fueled both of their addictions to alcohol. How my mother got her heroin was another story of pain that impacted me in catastrophic ways for years.

What I thought was a wonderful time in such a beautiful place would turn out to be a tool Evil used against our family. Our two years in Rio introduced my mother to the enemies who would eventually fuel a final victory over her. I did not know how the same victory celebration was planned for my father and me for a long time. Of course, the same was intended for my wife and our descendants. At least, that was the enemy's plan.

Knowing such a plan existed against my family fueled my determination to help others learn how to defend themselves. It fueled my passion for leading my family to sacred and protected ground.

In 1983, I became clean from drugs and alcohol. You will learn how I went further down that road than even my mother. Today, sharing how to avoid fighting most battles is my goal. Today, I know how to win battles because I lost so many.

A Study of the Enemy's Tactics

By now, you have heard some of the names of the agents of harm used repeatedly. We allow these influencers to take up residence in our lives without fear of the damage they will cause. Learning to become more alert when they surface will reduce their damage in our lives. So, let's talk more about the strategy of the enemy, with the caveat that there are many variations of these tactics.

Each attack against us focuses on our situations or weaknesses. More alarmingly, each frontal attack then summons more harmful enemies to enter through the smallest of holes in the walls of our lives until they burst wide open.

This campaign of deceit can be recognized by the tactics used. Below are the constant attackers found so far in my story. Some of these are common to us all. The order they follow and the frequency of their attacks change as they learn how we react (or don't react) to their presence.

Phase 1 Strategy: Sneak Attacks

Distraction, diversion, destruction, depression, disruption, lies, confusion, pain, anger—Evils like these should always be easy to recognize. The first enemy to breach our walls invites another who specializes in stealth. For example, the enemy confusion analyzes his campaign's effectiveness, analyzes our other weaknesses, and asks the next warrior to attack through that weakness. Confusion and distraction often strike our clarity of thought (peace) and invite indecision to join them. This attack plan often succeeds without us ever knowing we are under attack!

Phase 2 Strategy: A Siege against Us

While each person will have a customized battle plan used against them, you can count on more than one phase of an attack.

Seemingly harmless enemies arrive as soon as possible. For me, loneliness came years after the war against me started. Loneliness is often not recognized as a bad influence. It and others count on that fact. But if you understand there will be *no* loneliness in our eternal reward in heaven, then you can count on the fact that loneliness is unhealthy. See Matthew 5:12, Matthew 6:19–20, Luke 6:23, and 1 Corinthians 3:14.

At some time and as early as possible, the more harmful enemies arrived to attack my mother and me: immorality, sexual evil, abuse, infidelity, and others.

Phase 2 sees more damaging and often "hidden" Evils take up residence in our lives. It is also a goal to make us comfortable with this Evil. For the youngest years of my life, Phase 2 was working well.

Phase 3: Evil Comes Out into the Open

Some Evil is much more noticeable and easy to spot. In addition, these Evils are ones that none of us want to be around. So, they wait until their homes in our lives are well built and ready for them to move in.

Violence, drug abuse, and alcohol abuse often are used as frontal attacks. They rarely hide their attack plans. At this stage of the war against us, it is expected we will give up and give in.

Phase 4: Permanent Residents

The ultimate goal of all attacks is to remove us as a threat to Evil. The enemy fears our impact. He also sees our potential more than we do, which annoys him since he can never be blessed as we can.

Permanent pain, incarceration, and brain damage through lifestyle abuse all strive to become permanent companions. These are only a few of the permanent goals planned for us. Then finally, death and eternal separation from heaven becomes his war prize!

It will help if you also appreciate how Evil never gives up and will try new tactics. For me, impatience attacks me often today. Yes, impatience is a sin, and yes, that makes me a sinner. This sin strikes me often, and I must go to my Lord Jesus for forgiveness and rescue on a daily basis!

Distraction and diversion have both flooded the writing of my books for years, but peace has stayed with me and is stronger than the enemies. Yes, battles will always be likely, but peace, hope, and joy are more potent than all the enemies. During your battles, make it a primary goal to seek after these allies!

Success has also been a distraction in my writing. It is one of the forces that can be used for good or bad. My counsel is to surround yourself with healthy resources and take the time to evaluate every visitor to your life, whether human or supernatural. Especially be alert when you become comfortable with your successes.

I have known for far too long how late I am in finishing this book. Work-related success distracted and delayed me often. Whenever I try to write, work-related opportunities arrive to distract me. Success is an attractive distraction for me and many others.

In addition, several infrequent events came along to slow or stop me. They diverted my attention away from writing. They were distractions that hoped to delay or destroy. I see where they came from, and they are now in the past. Those enemies have been forced to retreat, but they attacked again just before I wrote these words!

Could it be evil Satan himself feared this chapter? Yes!

How Do We Guard Our Doorways?

The destinations my mother chose to frequent contributed to the losses she would encounter later. The same was true for me. How do we learn to avoid visiting the wrong places before they take their toll on our happiness? How do we know not to step through a doorway that is bad for us before we enter?

I have tried to answer this question by searching for the exact entry point where misery initially entered my mother's life. The primary influencer for each destination may have been depression, but did the places she visited also influence her demise? Yes is the undoubted answer, but her life traveled many roads and made many destination choices.

Misdirection works to rob us of an answer. Misdirection works closely with the enemy named gamble. Together, they coached us into believing we should try a new destination and only then evaluate how healthy it was. This "burn and learn" testing of a new place is very wrong!

Misdirection also wants us to deal with symptoms of problems instead of working on the causes. You can expect a distraction aimed at keeping you from ever realizing the dangers by feeding you false pleasures to distract you from seeing the threat.

We should guard our doorways by evaluating each destination before we enter. Please understand I am not talking about living in bad neighborhoods. Many good people have neighbors living in sin. Instead, I am talking about places we choose to visit where Evil is known to thrive.

Mother poorly chose some destinations where Evil found it easy to expand its reach into her soul. I can name some of the enemies and places that won victories against her and me, but tracing the enemy's complete and exact battle plan is not easy, and documenting all such sites is impossible.

Instead, I offer some uncomplicated advice. The advice is to avoid dealing with the symptoms of a wrong choice and learn to evaluate what a journey to a destination can cause *before* entering the doorway. Mother blindly walked into *Trouble Traps* and had to deal with the symptoms. I made similar mistakes.

I also learned the hard way how a healthy crossing guard stood at the beginning of each of my poor direction choices. This "life coach" stood ready to offer sound advice, but the clutter I surrounded myself with either drowned out his or her voice or distractions lured me into trouble.

We must also never forget why Evil attacks us. He sees we can become people of peace and love, things he can never have. He knows we can promote Good to others, and we can be healed and forgiven. He hates who he can never be and what he can never have! He works to lure us away from good decisions and healthy places.

I have learned how my own bad choices of paths to follow fueled my pain and worries. Yes, we step through doorways and into sin, and temptation never gives up on baiting us!

I also see how choosing the correct option at other crossroads took me on blessed pathways. Today, I am surrounded by a wife, children, and grandchildren at the center of my earthly peace. This better journey began when I learned to avoid wrong turns and how to choose healthy ones.

I must add that many other people stood at the entry to my crossroads and pointed the way to the good turns. Some I saw, some I ignored, and others I was distracted from seeing. While I can't list them all, mentioning some of them can help others slow down and analyze where each turn they are about to make could lead. It is also important to realize how after a wrong turn, there is often a path back to the right turn. The story of my life is proof of this. If I can come back from my past, anyone can do the same! Also, note that standing at my crossroads ready to help were often strangers. These earthly agents were there standing, prepared to "pay it forward."

Let me share an example. In high school, I struggled with math. Joy Long sat beside me in class. I barely knew her, but she offered to help me. Why? It was not romantic. Instead, she was born of generationally blessed parents and brothers. It was in their character to "guide." She stepped forward to help, and I almost missed her offer.

Joy Long stood silently in my doorway. She and others stand quietly, ready to offer guidance. The enemy works to distract us away from such life coaches!

Another point to mention is that those life coaches who stand in our doorways will often show up more than once. It was not their plan to do so. Joy would later become my sister-in-law when she married my wife's brother, Mike Lemmons. Some would say this was a coincidence. I see it as the will of our Lord Jesus Christ.

Michele Lemmons, Joy Long Lemmons, Mike & Stacey Lemmons

Havens of Peace and Hope

Some places radiate peace. Before my mother died, I had brief visits to healthy places filled with generationally blessed people. Visits to her sister Annette Gambrell Edwards and my father's sister Barbara Stewart Glenn were examples. These homes and others introduced me to hope I would only fully realize years later. Dysfunctional lifestyles like my family had were not present in these homes.

Then there was the haven of hope that would become my next home. My earliest memories of my grandmother, Blanche Stewart Lee, come from when I was seven years old. In Greer, South Carolina, her home covered more than two acres of land and would eventually become a place of protected peace for me.

Grandma Blanche Hall Stewart Lee and Grandpa Oscar Lee

My father had played a vital role in the building of this home place years before my birth. He also worked with my grandmother to turn these grounds into a kind of city park environment. Dad knew how to fix more than looms in the cotton mill. He also learned how to build places of peace. Father knew what places of peace were. Trading that for the life he lived with my mother indeed must have torn at him.

In my brief visits there, I saw a place that was in color—full, beautiful color. There were two sizeable in-ground goldfish ponds, and there were flowers of all types everywhere. Church groups and other families would come to picnic and enjoy this wonderful place. There was an abundance of trees and hills to climb and apples to eat. My grandmother had a green thumb and even used to run a nursery next to her home. A spring-fed creek ran through the property and had cut deep into and through massive granite at one place. Dad built a concrete dam across here to create a natural pond. There were many types of trees, including weeping willows.

There were numerous places in her haven where I had many happy memories. Areas can grow peace, and here it was easy to find. This sacred ground was not noisy. Nature could be heard. This place was unlike any I had experienced before.

Here, I learned to appreciate nature and greatly loved my time at Grandma's haven. Meals at her house were another special blessing. Love and care took on an exceptional value in this place. This place put my young soul at peace, but each time, we were only visiting.

As I look back on the crossroads of my life, I see places that fueled such happiness and other areas that did not. This place was one of peace where enemies like sadness were not welcome. Here I learned how there are places of refuge where I could find shelter from life's storms. Soon this place would become my haven. For a while, though, I could only visit. Have I told you yet that sadness is not a good force?

Before the days living at my grandmother's wonderland, we lived nearby in Greenville, South Carolina. Dad always worked in the textile industry, so we often rented homes near enough to his job to enable him to walk to work. During the time my mother was alive, I never remember us having a car. How my mother was able to travel to support her bad lifestyle habits would also become a curse.

We sometimes visited my mother's brothers' and sisters' homes, who also lived in Greer, South Carolina. At Uncle Ralph Gambrell's house, I learned to compete. His youngest son Danny and I were the same age. While they visited inside, Danny and I would go outside and wrestle. We always wrestled to a draw. Anger never came, just competition. Years later, I would use this skill in some beneficial athletic ways. The bond between Danny, his brothers, and our cousins has lasted. That choice of people to associate with was a good one. The Gambrell home was also a place of hope.

Cousin Danny Gambrell

All my cousins and their families are also fierce competitors and stand united to accomplish their goals. Competition is a force that can be good or bad. My cousins used it for good. For a time, I used it to promote my Evil.

During my troubled years, I often needed a lighthouse to show me the way. The Gambrell siblings and their cousins all maintained a strength of character that came from quality parental influences. They always knew the safe roads to travel, and they all excelled accordingly. They also had something I had not yet appreciated—integrity. It would take me many years to learn to have integrity. My time with this family started me on that journey.

There were also times when we visited the home of my brother. After each visit, my mother's depression worsened. I remember how just before each visit, Mom was always happy. Afterward, depression returned and worsened. Separation can be good or bad. Joy was evident while my mother was with my brother. Knowing what to separate ourselves from takes a lot of wisdom Mother simply did not have.

The secret my mother kept from my brother fed her misery. Can secrets be judged as evil influences? Are secrets the beginning of deception that will turn into lies? Yes! Evil often starts subtly and slowly creeps into misery. Then other Evils like destruction and death surface. Much of this Evil lasts throughout a lifetime. It also works to destroy families and has considerable skills at this goal.

Diversion, deception, misdirection, then lies—these forces attack our integrity. Destroying our integrity is a primary goal of our enemies. Why? Integrity builds trust, and trust builds faith.

The journeys that start with a slight mistake do grow with each new footstep. Good news comes in the knowledge that simply understanding this can alert us when our path is difficult before becoming lost on the trail.

I pray the home my brother grew up in was his haven.

How do we find healthy places and people? For me, this was not possible during the years with my mother. As adults, we can exercise some control over our environment and places of peace and security for ourselves and our children. Before I was an adult, I was forced to travel to places where misery loved company instead. For a time, I thought this lifestyle was normal.

Confusion, separation, and distraction all work against you ever seeing places of hope or peace. When you approach a healthy haven of hope, the enemy knows it before you do. He will rob you of these havens by attacking your relationship with the hosts of such places.

Monitor the words coming out of the mouths of people around you. If their words are not words of peace, joy, or hope, then they have none of this in their lives, so keep looking.

If noise drowns out your ability to think clearly, keep looking for a different place. Or, if a place you visit is full of people without peace, then keep looking.

In summary, a place of peace is a place where nature is the loudest sound you hear.

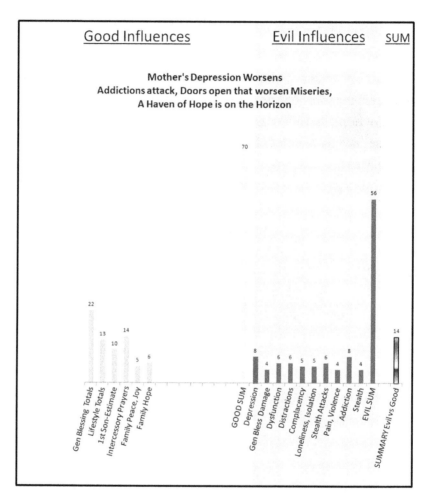

Good Influences   Evil Influences   SUM

Mother's Depression Worsens
Addictions attack, Doors open that worsen Miseries,
A Haven of Hope is on the Horizon

More ground is lost, but hope is on the horizon.

A Miraculous Deathbed Intercession

W here we lived when my mother died was close to many havens of hope. It was also close to places that bred destruction. I learned at an early age how visiting healthy sites filled with healthy people was not an everyday practice for our family. The atmosphere around my home was a far cry from that of my grandmother's home.

I learned too late that joy and peace often came from being around people of hope. Is it possible that Jesus himself would also deliver an intercessory miracle of hope to us, to my family? Let us review the death of my mother to arrive at the answer.

Miracles do abound today. They are everywhere! Keeping us from believing in miracles is a significant part of a plan to rob us of many blessings such as peace. Sadly, miracles are not something we can always call for like we can for a video on demand. Sometimes people pray for intercession in the lives of other people. Sometimes it is for loved ones; other times, it is for strangers. Through this intercessory action, miracles can occur, and yes, angels are often the delivery method.

People often give up on asking our Creator for help when their "rescue me" prayers are not favorably answered or on the timetable we demand. Intercession happens, and most of the time, we don't even realize it. I learned of the power of intercession after it was too late to thank in person most of those who asked for my intercessions.

You will soon read of horrible things that happened while I traveled with my mother through her most evil and troubled journeys, but she asked for and was granted intercession that changed my life and will hopefully, prayerfully, impact yours as well.

I speak of peace often. I offer praise that I have it and have had it for years. I also talk about how deception is an Opposing Agent that works to rob us. On Easter Sunday 2020, I finally understood I did not have total peace and was being deceived about a crucial part of my past.

I only had partial peace. There was something in me that had never found peace. The incredible peace I have had pleased me to the point where I thought I needed no more. This partial peace caused me to ignore one crucial fact: *I had never forgiven my mother.* This distraction had won a victory over me for years!

Yes, I learned how the Evil my mother introduced into my life could become less painful, and I could evolve away from those memories and into partial peace. Yes, I verbally criticized my mother, even from the pulpit. I used the great Evil she surrounded me with as an introduction to getting the attention of people I hoped to reach. I am sure they realized I had yet not forgiven her. They were correct.

I constantly used the "shock and awe" of only tiny bits of her past (and mine) to open doors. It always got people's attention, but they could tell I had no love or forgiveness for her.

On Easter morning 2020, I woke early and prayed to my Savior Jesus Christ and thanked him for his sacrifice and the blessings I have received through him. I asked for forgiveness of all my sins. That morning, he finally got through to me that I had to forgive my mother. Finally, after years of living the lie that I had total peace, I knew I had not. I had become satisfied with partial peace. Peace can continue to grow throughout our lives. It can also increase our joy as it grows. See Matthew 28:5–6, Luke 24:6–7, Acts 4:33, and John 11:25–26.

The Lord Jesus placed into my understanding that Easter morning the details of what happened just before my mother died—things I already knew but had not yet devoted adequate prayer time to ask why or fully understand. We do not always get instant answers when praying for peace. Sometimes we do and yet choose to think otherwise. Instead of analyzing the final details of her life as any good problem-solving fixer would do, I ignored them. I hardened my heart to think otherwise.

On that morning in January 1963, my father knew she was again using drugs and asked me to stay home from my third-grade class to be with her while he went to work. Her heroin and other drug use were common, so he decided to risk going to work. I have never blamed him for leaving us that day because he had navigated through these crossroads many times before.

Dad had once lived in a haven of peace when he lived with my grandmother. Years later, that peace was only a distant memory I am sure was canceled by pain brought on by my mother's Evil, but he never gave up on her. He loved her even through her most evil days.

Before lunch, my mother was unconscious. I went to the bus stop in front of our home and asked a stranger for help. I told her I was afraid that my mother was dying. The woman said she had to go to work and got on the bus. That day, my faith in people took a dark turn that would last for many years. This incident also attacked my trust in people and welcomed loneliness to fill the void. That bus-stop battle was a victory won against me.

Trust is mandatory in a relationship with the Lord Jesus. Accordingly, we can be assured it will come under attack.

I called my father's older sister Audrey Rector, who promptly came to the rescue. Aunt Audrey would also become the agent of rescue for me many times in the future. Her home became another place of hope and peace. Her children also became friends I greatly needed. Through her, miracles of intercession would come to my rescue during some of my most troubled years. I never lost trust in Aunt Audrey. She never gave up on me. She often stood in harm's way to do right by me.

The diagnosis for my mother was that she would never wake up and that her time left was just a few hours. She hung on for days and even had moments when she mumbled a word or two. One night while just she and my father were present, and while not wholly aware of her surroundings and incapable of carrying on a conversation, she said, "Bible." My father placed one on her chest and put her hand on it. I am told her facial expression changed to one of peace!

Hours later, she was mumbling something to someone who was not there. Dad asked her who she was talking to, and she made the only coherent reply she made while lying in that hospital bed. She said one word: Jesus!

The doctors talked about what a miracle it was she could even reply to a question. Hope had arrived, but it did not last. Hope came for my purpose, but it took years before I understood it.

Soon they were taking her for a new x-ray when a male nurse jerked the pillow out from under her head for the x-ray. Her head fell back hard onto the gurney, and she instantly passed away. My trust in people once again came under attack. This attack intended to separate me from ever trusting in people in the healing professions again, which worked for a while.

At this point, I hope to counsel readers how a continued attack against a value in our lives often signals an area where a future blessing will be. *We can measure attacks against trust as a place where the Fallen Angel fears how we will see that resource blossom in our future!* There are other areas where the same thoughts apply.

I boast how I am a problem solver equaled by few. I brag how I am a nationally known expert on and designer of smart house technology. As brilliant as I think I am and while often gloating as the great fixer of smart houses, I had overlooked what was happening in that hospital. I ignored how sometime before I was born, my mother had learned where to ask for the only intercession that mattered, heaven-sent intercession. She knew this from her mother, LuVadie Lawson Gambrell, and her other Gambrell siblings.

Mother also grew up in a family atmosphere where Jesus was not a stranger. She knew Jesus, and he still loved her even though her sin had ruled her life. This truth applies to all of us. See Romans 5:8, Colossians 3:13, and Matthew 18:21–22.

Although I don't remember any talk of Jesus Christ while my mother was alive, she had prepared for her death. She asked for two songs to sing that assured me she knew Jesus before lying on her deathbed. Those songs were "The Old Rugged Cross" and "When the Roll is Called Up Yonder." If you are not familiar with those songs, listen to them. The words of both songs indicate my mother loved our Lord, even before her last moment on earth.

What did she say to Jesus on her deathbed? He was there beside her; she had asked him to be there, and he was. Until that Easter morning, I had overlooked why. She was admitting her sinful life and asking for forgiveness. She knew her wrongs, and even in a drug-induced coma with a blood clot in her brain, she sought forgiveness and received one last chance.

Is a last chance deathbed intercession promised to others? Is the last chance always granted on the hospital bed? Sadly, no, but we have many opportunities to find true peace we ignore long before our final moment.

That deathbed intercession came not just for her. It also came for me. It also opens the door for readers to find this peace before they find themselves on their own deathbeds!

Even in a life filled with sin, you can still be forgiven. Just don't count on waiting until you see death coming for you! You can depend on forgiveness for the asking, no matter what your sin is. The only qualifier is believing in the Lord Jesus, asking him into your life, and asking for forgiveness. See Romans 10:9 and Romans 6:23.

Up until that Easter morning, I lived with the fact that my mother's lifestyle had permanently separated her from Jesus and me. I was wrong. I now know she awaits my father and me. All the Evil we experience will have no presence in heaven, and they will cease to exist. When we finally meet again, we will have no memories of past mistakes. Now that's heaven! See Matthew 6:14.

I also now know she asked for intercession for me to not walk in her footsteps. Others prayed for intercession for me, but I can now add my mother to that list. That Easter's sermon was from my close friend and pastor Mark Smith at Mt. Lebanon Baptist Church, and along with the songs directed by Minister of Music Ted Conwell, both spoke directly to my heart. That day, I forgave my mother. That day signaled an even more profound peace in my life.

Bottom: Mount Lebanon Baptist Church, 572 Mt. Lebanon Church Rd. Greer, SC 29651; Top: Pastor Mark Smith, Minister of Music Ted Conwell

Please don't take this event as permission to wait until your deathbed to reach out. It may not come. It probably won't come. Early in my mother's life, she had learned from her family the eternal peace that trusting Jesus brings. She made that vital decision early in life. Although she abandoned peace and chose to follow Evil, the fact she had earlier decided to choose Jesus permanently qualified her to enter heaven.

That deathbed intercession was not just for her. It was for me, my brother, and my father. It was an example of true mercy.

I finally realized this was a factor of discipline. It took discipline to put myself in places where the message could be delivered through people of peace. Pastor Mark and Minister of Music Ted provide that kind of message daily. It took years to realize they were speaking healing to me. Chances are, they never knew their sermons or the music was talking directly to me. Instead, they just had the discipline to minister.

Today, I hear from our Lord through their voices a lot more frequently. Hearing a message from our Lord through a sermon or song is common. He also uses many other methods to reveal himself.

This morning, just before I began to write, I turned on some Christian music. Immediately, the song "Mercy Walked In" by Gordon Mote played. Timely huh? That's the way our Lord works. We must only start looking for his hand!

Understanding the purpose of the last-minute intercession for my mother has allowed me to appreciate better the numerous rescues that came my way after her death.

Those rescues were not just for me. I write to inspire others who have also lost much and think forgiveness is hopeless. Start listening for words from our Savior. They will undoubtedly come through pastors like Mark Smith and Ted Conwell, but there are many pipelines the Lord uses to send such messages of hope.

Mother's sins were profound, but she had chosen Jesus. She wasted years of her life, but her heavenly Father still called her his child and welcomed her home. She gave birth to this book. Her prayers of intercession for her descendants that came through me continue to protect her other descendants and me.

The intensity of the evil *Trouble Traps* in front of us is related to how much the Fallen Angel Satan fears us. That's right, and he sees how the creator God smiles on us through his son Jesus. So he sends misery and all its companions to lure us into the wrong paths. I know this because I have seen too many incredibly talented people fall victim to his traps.

He saw how one day my words would spare at least one from walking the journey of misery. The master of Evil thought he could stop me from writing these words by destroying my mother. He was wrong yet again!

Again, *we can always measure the trueness of our course in life by the amount of evil opposition to it!* A single person can positively impact the world no matter how much they have struggled. This fact is proven true over and over.

The death and horrible circumstances that caused my mother's death could have quickly hardened my heart past the point of healing. For a season, the enemy Satan won that fight, but my losses were not to be a permanent victory. Through the life and death of my mother, inspiration created this book. As a result of this story, at least one reader will find eternal life. Today, my mother is now on my all-time list of heroes. She opened the door. I only write about it. Intercession is a powerful resource!

This battle plan against me that included the death of my mother was lost, but the wars against my father, brother, and me were not over. Evil saw how someone in my future would find healing in our story and grow past their losses to become an inspiration to others in need of healing and peace. Satan has worked hard to stop anyone from hearing this story.

Evil meant to ruin me and almost stole my mother, but he lost both of those wars. His victory over my mother was only during her earthly life. He lost on his plan to rob her of eternal peace and joy.

In my case, he won some significant victories and will continue to attack me until I join with my mother and father in eternal glory. Somehow, this story will reach one or more who have walked similar journeys as them and me. Is that one person you or someone you love?

I dare not challenge the Fallen One personally, but when the evil one next attacks, I promise to call on the name of Jesus Christ as my protector. Each time Evil wins a skirmish, I will become even more determined to reveal his strategy to others.

In addition, his constant attacks have taught me to realize how negative impacts and influences *do not* come from my Lord! Accordingly, he will lose many battles before they root themselves in my life. Hallelujah! Negativity previously went unnoticed, but no longer.

Distractions and Interruptions

I offer these short words to illustrate how the Fallen One severely attacked me over the previous chapter. The content in that chapter bothered him so much he sent numerous distractions and interruptions to keep me from sharing it.

The enemy never totally gives up! He loves to interrupt hope, joy, and peace and distract us toward Evil. Surprise attacks come in unexpected ways. You can predict they will come when the Fallen One sees he will lose ground because of your efforts.

To stop or impact its words, distraction brought interruption, confusion, aggravation, and delays to attack the contents in the previous thoughts. They hit all at once and with a lot of energy!

Example: As I wrote, we were expecting the delivery of a new refrigerator. A mistake made by the supplier caused a delay I learned about just before the delivery time. To resolve this mistake took hours to solve and required an in-person visit to the store.

We planned to have two refrigerators during this time. Why? My daughter Melanie and husband Patrick are living with us while they build a new home next door. Before the sale of their home can be finalized, they must also provide a new refrigerator for that home as theirs had a broken ice-maker. Upon delivery of their new refrigerator, they found it was damaged beyond repair in shipping. Both distractions came at the same time.

Patrick & Melanie Stewart Henson

Hours later, I am back to writing. Instead of being defeated, I was able to use this interruption to illustrate how spiritual warfare works. Oh yes, the issues with the refrigerators are still not solved, but these delays created good examples of how even small things can be used to attack our peace! Pay attention when interruptions and distractions come. There are no deliveries from heaven with either of those names!

Then, right before I was ready to finalize these words, another distraction came. An alarm siren inside our outside storage building sounded. When I stopped to evaluate this noise, I learned the siren goes off even when the alarm is disarmed. Since 1976, our family business has installed alarm systems. I know alarm systems, and this one had no logical reason for going off—that is until you realize inanimate objects can also be used to distract us.

Too often, we pay little or no attention to such things. Never overlook distractions. They may be present to divert you away from new blessings headed your way and even cause physical harm.

Evil I Lived With

What I share now includes the last few years of my mother's life. It must be told because I occasionally hear from people how their past is so horrible they can have no future hope. Wrong! If I can make it through these horrors, anyone can.

Once, when speaking to a group of teenaged boys who were imprisoned due to committing adult crimes, I was asked by one why "rescues" like mine did not come for him.

This question came from a fifteen-year-old boy who would most likely spend most of his life in prison. I struggled to come up with an answer.

Today, I say that rescues come to the crossroads of our past because of what we will do in our future. Jesus knew I would one day ask him if I could play a role in promoting peace and hope for his children. This intercession can happen for you. Decide you will serve, and miracles can also come your way!

Jesus also knew years before I would ask for intercession for my family what I would ask for on their behalf. You see, one day, I looked at the face of my wife Kim and saw a blessing beyond measure. I knew my life of Evil had to change. I then looked at Anthony, my son, and Melanie, my daughter, and realized I would generationally curse their lives unless I changed my future.

On that day of reckoning, I asked Jesus to help me become a leader who could wisely lead my family to him, and that prayer was answered. The generational curse I began life with has become a generational blessing for them and my grandchildren Colin, Jewel, Zoie, and Emma.

To successfully reach the most hopeless of lost souls, I must share the horrors of my past. I share not to glorify any of these events at all. Instead, I choose to illustrate how your past can be forgiven and forgotten, no matter what happened.

When I first wrote this chapter, it was not suitable for all readers. The things that happened needed to be softened. This chapter is the amended words of those years.

Those days with my mother were a principal factor in my desire to lead my family away from Evil. No one should live through such times to arrive at peace. However, not all of us are born under the care of God-fearing people. So, I offer the horrors and following rescues of my past to provide hope for your future.

For the last two years of my mother's life, I accompanied her as she reacted to her depression. I learned sin firsthand. The results were that I grew past my years of childhood and into a world few survive. At age seven, my childhood ended when her depression took her to dark places and forced me to go along.

I became content with dysfunction. It took the constant attacks of numerous evil soldiers to convince me dysfunction was acceptable. This agent of harm robs us of our sense of normality. It succeeds when we accept an unnatural lifestyle as normal. I had to live inside a dysfunctional environment. I was only seven years old. Dysfunction was but one of the Evils I walked beside. At least for a time, this was my life.

Before my children turned seven, I had to change their futures. Evil's plan was for them and Kim to follow my evil trail. Evil's goal was for them to become like Evil Me!

Contentment. Is that a happy and healthy place to be? Is contentment a word we can always count on to be good and healthy for us? It's easy to realize the term dysfunction is never good, but place contentment beside dysfunction, and together they lie to us that their presence is acceptable. That was my early life. I was content to live a dysfunctional life!

Mother was a beautiful woman. That, too, was used against her. She attracted men, and once they came close, Evil took hold of both of them while I was present.

Betty Gambrell Stewart (mother), Harry Donald Stewart (father)

I was content to go with my mother when she was unfaithful to my father and when she used heroin, and I was with her when she used desperate measures to pay for the drugs and her lifestyle. Her beauty must have easily opened the door to evil men. Some of these evil men insisted she hide their sins from me. Others were content for me to watch. Others wanted my participation.

I became content with sometimes being locked out in the cold while she was unfaithful to my father. I was content when I spent nights away from my home with her and various evil men.

I can't say I was content when I was locked outside one cold day and jumped off the porch of some man's home and onto a board with a nail in it that ran entirely through my right foot. I began to learn this kind of distorted contentment often came with pain of all types. However, it was my life and the only thing I knew. I had no way to change things, so the lie of contentment came to live with me through those days. While these days hurt me, I did not realize they were wrong. It became normal for me to accept dysfunction.

Later, during my years as a police officer, I could spot this enemy in the homes of many I encountered. I spared many from jail in hopes an inspirational speech from me could make a difference. Sadly, I was wrong too often, but mediation did come for some.

During my time with my mother, I learned how regular eating was also not an everyday occurrence. When we were away from my father, I remember hunger as a frequent companion. Hunger was not a visitor when with my father. His work ethic and devotion to my mother and me never let us miss a meal. Yes, we were poor, but dad's work ethic gave us the basics. How he continued to support us through these years amazes me today. How he continued to allow her back into our home is also a mystery. That he continued to support us both made him the hero he still is to me today. Finally, years later, I would learn how true love like his also comes with forgiveness.

Once locked outside, cold and hungry, I could not get my mother to come to the door of the man's house where we were. Earlier that day, this man had hoped to buy my favor by giving me a pocket knife that I then used to silently cut through a screen window of this man's home. I raised the window, pushed the curtain aside, and peered into his bedroom. No child should ever see the things I saw through that window.

I did not eat that day. That pocket knife would be the only gift any of her men ever offered me. Instead, the things they awarded me were not prizes. During these two years, I learned to lie and deceive my father. In later years, that same knife would also find an evil purpose.

There were times when my mother drugged me to mask the things she did with other men. Occasionally, the drugs she would use would paralyze me, but I could still hear what was happening in the same room where I was supposedly asleep.

My childhood ended, and life grew worse. Yes, I knew Evil through my mother. Together, we walked those roads. Mother by choice, me by association. Those experiences affected my ability to forgive her for years.

Contentment can take on a dangerous false feeling of normality. I honestly did not know right from wrong. Accordingly, my future was doomed, and, of course, my childhood had ended prematurely. Years later, as a police officer, I saw many examples of these crimes against nature and children. My heart broke each time. The desire to help, and not by incarceration, grew within me. One day, that desire would see me lose my job when the ACLU attacked me for my efforts while in uniform.

Many children are living in dysfunctional homes who only see hope at school or in church. Today, their sense of right is falling victim even in some schools. There was a time when schools taught principles that worked to eliminate the "causes" of problems. The morals of our ancestors saw to that. Today, too many schools are forced to work on the symptoms instead.

My daughter Melanie taught in middle school for years. She acted as a fixer and reached some children who, like me, had an unhealthy home. Is this still possible to do in our schools today? Teachers still exist in these environments, but do they live in fear of being disciplined? Could there be a subtle attack today against such values?

In class, intercessory prayer must now take an even more remote stance. Evil now walks the unprotected halls of too many public schools today. Our ancestors did not see this day coming.

Contentment is an influence that works to make us adapt to our surroundings, good or bad.

Unseen Battles for Our Future

Soon after my mother's death, I would meet a new variation of contentment. While Mother was alive, I had no idea the battle for my future was raging. Most days, I lived a horrible hidden life, but other people had prayers for my future in their hearts. I was still content in a dysfunctional manner, but another plan was underway.

Grandpa Willet Oscar Lee was my step-grandfather. However, he invested in me as if I were of his blood. Grandpa married my grandmother Blanche after my grandfather John Stewart fell dead of a heart attack in his barbershop in downtown Greer. This happened years before my birth.

I never knew Grandpa Stewart, but I can tell from the depth of good character rooted in his two daughters and two sons that he was a man of integrity—spiritually sound integrity. Had he lived, I know he would have also been a powerful influence on my father, mother, and me. He was an ancestor who built generational blessings.

Grandpa Lee was the one who showed me the happier side of contentment. He eagerly stepped into the role of a strong leader for me. Grandpa Lee was known as Uncle Oscar by many and was a big sports fan. He had been a supervisor in the textile industry where my grandmother worked. He noticed her beauty, both inside and out, and married her. He was a wise man in many ways, and he had a plan for me.

Mom Dies, Dad Leaves

After my mother's sudden death in early January 1963, my dad quickly took a job as a fixer in Africa in the town of Aba, Nigeria. He chose a new country as the way to deal with the loss of my mother. In a short time, I had lost both parents, and I was living with my grandparents. The hills around her home became my next "Miracle Hills." My angel of comfort this time would be my precious grandmother, Blanche Charity Stewart Lee. Others were soon to follow. The Evil I had lived with was being replaced.

New enemies came to attack me, but they dared not draw attention to themselves. Subtle enemies attacked instead. Loneliness led the charge, with confusion and separation close behind. Today, I wish I could see the hidden battles that raged between those evil liars and the angels sent by my prayer warriors to fight for my future. When those enemies tried to cross the boundaries of grandmother's haven, the battles must have been fierce!

Somehow, I had never yet learned to hate. That would soon change too.

Mother's deathbed experience began a new journey for me. Her intercession was instrumental in ways that would eventually change my life for the better, but first, I had to learn to cope with my new companions of misery.

With my mom dead and my dad in Africa, lonely came to visit again, but the countless evil influences that had been my constant companions before were not welcome in my new home. Grandpa Lee and Grandma Blanche Charity Lee stood guard at those gates.

But lonely was a previous companion, and he snuck quietly past the gates and into this new haven.

I had made a real friend at my previous home. Her name was Peggy. She is my earliest memory of a friend, and we walked to school together each day. That friendship was as close as I had ever come to genuine companionship. I never saw Peggy again. Separation and loneliness grew more assertive in my new home. For a time, I thought about her often.

Loneliness intended to rob me of healthy relationships, but it also brought on incredible blessings. For the first time, I began to notice the bonds between other healthy families. My father's sister Barbara Glenn had a family I admired. The same was true for his other sister, Audrey Rector. Nearby, wholesome influences were plentiful.

Soon after the move, Grandpa Lee took me to his church, Victor Methodist. I met Chris Dumas, Robbie M., Judy O., and others with families with a value system new to me. A change came fast—one that showed me a new world of families. I began to see a new world of relationships I wanted in my own life. I also learned to respect Jesus Christ and all who spoke his name favorably. Even before I was a Christian myself, I respected him. This fact alone spared me the sin of attacking Christians. Respect—now there's a valuable character trait!

These friends soon replaced the loneliness I felt about Peggy. Peggy, today I pray for you, and in my prayers, I ask we will be able to walk the streets again one day in our eternity.

Is change good or bad? I needed change, significant change. Changes did arrive. Some were good, others not so good. I began to be content again, but this time, contentment felt good! True contentment is good, but there is a liar who also claims contentment as his name. He had fooled me for too long. Once I began to learn from my new influences, I started a long journey of healing. The

Gambrells, Glenns, Stewarts, Rectors, and my new church family all played crucial roles in my journey to normal.

Change can also be part of a lie we accept and breeds a false sense of security. Is peace always a good thing? Yes! Evil falsely generated contentment in my young years, but peace never came. There was peace here in this new home and life, and love also arrived and had a powerful presence. Real contentment was in this place, and so was a new kind of love.

With my move to my grandparents' home, I quickly began to see the world in a brand new way. Peace, joy, happiness, and all of their friends were always nearby. Those memories are in full and beautiful living color today. The memory of being locked outside in the cold remains, but in shades of gray.

Learning the true character of people is key to continued happiness. The places they create and frequent can also be a mirror image of their hearts. When with my mother, I met men with no strength of character. I do not recall any of their faces, just their actions. Those men would not be present in this place I now called home.

At age nine, my life started over. Immediately I was surrounded by a lot of relatives and new friends who overwhelmed me with love. I had overlooked the importance of love to a large degree, but it took on a new meaning for me at my grandmother's home. Still, lonely dug in deep anyway, along with some of its subtle and well-hidden companions. They survived and grew inside this sacred place I now called home.

Before this move, I have no memory of ever hearing the words, "I love you." This missed emotion now changed in a hurry. This fact and several other mistaken beliefs were undergoing a conversion. People like these were the engine driving me toward healthy change.

When I moved in with my grandparents, I was in the third grade and needed to enroll in a new elementary school. Grandpa

Lee (Uncle Oscar) introduced me to his dear friend Mr. Smiley Williams, the principal at the nearby Victor Elementary School. Mr. Smiley and Grandpa played checkers and dominoes each day after school at the local hang-out, the Red Diamond gas station. The character of those "hang out" days were far removed from those I learned while dancing on the bar tops for money.

Mr. Smiley Williams in 1955

The healthy character of those who often met to play those games was new to me. I did not know then how often my future was discussed and plans made for me during their time of fellowship. These men would impact my life for many years to come. Intercession was scheduled for me again.

They saw a need and volunteered to fix it. Mr. Smiley was included in Grandpa's plan to battle the Evil that had filled my life, and he volunteered to lead several battlefronts and chose to stand in the gap for me.

Life Coaches

A t this point, I must dwell on an essential fact. People who care about us don't just pray general prayers for us. They ask our Lord for specific deliveries. It's easy to pray for someone you care about and ask for their protection, but prayers of a complex nature are also answered.

My intercessors and those sent to coach and guide me asked our Lord that I see a more regular and blessed life one day. They asked that I one day have a family as they had. They must have also been asking our Lord for me to start generational blessings for my future children. As unlikely as this was at the time they prayed, those prayers would be answered in abundance.

I never expected to be blessed by Kim Lemmons, but she arrived as an answer to those prayers. Today, our children Anthony and Melanie continue those blessings through their children, including Colin, Jewel, Zoie, and Emma. The generational blessing will continue through them.

Each of their life stories is already filled with many blessed victories. Those who prayed for my intercession must have asked for these measures of blessings to appear in abundance. The generational curses I was born into were broken. It may take many years or even several generations to happen, but specific prayers of intercession are answered. Prayer works!

Children should not have labels attached to them, but in my case, well before my mother died, I was already considered overly hyperactive and incapable of ever functioning normally. When I went to live with my grandparents, this disruptive force went with me. Today, I realize they sacrificed their peace for me that day. The same is true for the teachers and other students in my new third-grade class at Victor Elementary School. I was hard to handle, but intercessory prayers were being answered with this change of schools.

Disruption and hyperactivity are the names of enemies of peace and patience. The first step I took inside the door at Victor Elementary School signaled a new wave of battles for my future. These agents were fighting over me with each step I took up those stairs and into that building. I suspect similar war plans are put into place against us when we step into other such areas of hope. It was not me alone who took those steps. I had company—my family's prayers and even past ancestors went with me.

What would I see if I could have perceived the spiritual warfare going on as I climbed those stairs? Inside those walls were people with solid spirits of healing. The Fallen One knew this and sent a wave of Evil to overtake that place.

There were undoubtedly evil demons clinging to my body while soldiers of heaven fought them off. If I could put names on each of these warriors, what would they be? I have often desired to know the names of my guardian angels. One day, I will, but the thanks will be awarded to my Savior Jesus Christ. Still, I want to meet each of them and learn of their battles to fight for me.

The moment I entered this new place, a severe battle was most assuredly raging. The same is true for all of us as we approach such areas. Spiritual warfare is predictable! Expect it when you come near to what could be good for you.

In my desire to evaluate how I became disruptive at such a young age, I searched my past for a single event that fueled my annoying behavior. In the search for a single cause, I found no one thing. Instead, there were many chaotic events I lived through and all before I was nine years old. One by one, they worked together to turn my peace into chaos and hope into hopelessness.

It would be reasonable to assume the traumatic times with my mother were the sole cause of my behavior. This lifestyle I was forced to live was certainly a big factor but was not the only reason. The Fallen One also saw the prayer cover sent my way. He saw it from my ancestors and living prayer warriors. This sole fact caused him to fear leaving me alone.

When and if you begin to envision spiritual warfare around you, curiosity will paint some pictures for you. While I am confident Opposing Agents are aware intercessory prayers to the almighty God for our protection are happening, they can't hear their words at all. Instead, I think Righteous Prayers can knock them to the ground should they fly through one.

Another strength-building piece of advice I offer is to speak the name of Jesus Christ out loud and often. Expressing this builds boldness and makes him smile on you.

In later years when I served as a police officer, I occasionally was present when the spoken name of Jesus would cause a severe and violent reaction in some people. The exact details are left out and may appear in a future book about my years in uniform. For now, take note that Evil doesn't like to hear the name of Jesus and certainly can't be in the presence of prayers to him and his Holy Spirit! At the very least, know that prayers to Jesus are sacred and that the Opposing Agents fear them.

Life experiences while I walked beside my mother attacked places in my soul I never even knew existed. Loneliness invited uncertainty to join us. Our family knew these facts and most certainly accounted for intercessory prayers with my and my mother's names attached.

Once I moved in with my grandparents, a new misery often prompted me to ask, "Where is my mother?" Was she truly gone?

Why was she gone? Where and why became constant visitors. It was a couple of years after her death before I stopped seeing her in crowds. Why did my dad leave me behind? He had taken me to Brazil, so why not Africa? Denial also joined the misery team. Other evil influences would stay hidden until an advantageous time.

Uncertainty and denial were new to me. Nobody explained who these visitors were, and no one helped me understand them after they arrived. I was left to learn of them without any guidance. Uncertainty would replace trust, who had already been badly beaten, and denial would invite the evil liar to their team. Disruption attacked peace, intending to run my teachers out of patience. Lies alienated me from having new friends. Loneliness grew stronger.

But life coaches were already preparing to guide and protect me and my future. A long-range plan was also in place to one day introduce me to Kim Lemmons. Mr. Smiley knew us both long before we knew each other. The way our Lord works to bless us is far beyond my comprehension. Even after my time with Mr. Smiley in elementary school, our time together was not over.

Anger had not yet come to me, but it, too, would soon be included in this new battle plan against me, and it would bring powerful reinforcements, such as violence. What new things I would learn about competition would enable me to excel at sports and at the same time extend my anger. The competition I had known earlier was slowly expanding its presence in my life. Competition is an influence that, like contentment, can take on a good or bad character. It takes balance to use competition for good. I had not yet learned balance. Violence had a plan to overwhelm me, but it dared not do so while I was inside the protected haven of hope at my new home.

Evil analyzes our weaknesses and calls in the most appropriate enemy agent to attack next. By the same token, the agent angels of our Lord counters with other soldiers of Good. Competition became a healthy resource I have used throughout my life, but for too long, it also made me better at being bad.

A war plan always has a timeline and includes milestone goals. If the first wave does not achieve the desired goal, count on another one. The battles for my future immediately following my mother's death would be many and included new and powerful enemies that came in numerous waves of Evil.

You must understand that many of us give up and give in to our miseries with so many losses. Without sound coaching that includes the power of peace over disruption and joy over loneliness, hopelessness arrives! You are about to hear of some earthly volunteers who stepped onto the battlefield for me. Some I can name, others I cannot. The same is probably true for you.

My peaceful life in this new home would also come under attack. The Evil that had my name in its battle plan of destruction had to stay dormant but was not yet ready to give up. Many good influences now surrounded me, but I was slow to learn this.

Today, peace is a permanent place of joy for me. Evil still attacks, but I know who will have the final victory, and the attacks sent my way will one day be forgotten. A battle for hope is no longer a concern. Hope is now a permanent companion. This definition can fit inside the hearts of even the most defeated of souls. It is within reach. Evil will remain but will no longer dominate my life or yours.

Why would my life continue to be under such a fierce attack in my younger years? The answer is the same for all of us. Peace cannot be allowed to fill us with joy. Our future will include many blessings, and the Fallen Angel knows this. He can see if he loses battles against us, we could then touch the lives of others in powerful and healthy ways. He sees that we will "coach" some of the hopeless and lead them into a place of peace somewhere in our future. It is repeatedly proven that *the more severe the attack against us, the more the Fallen One fears our future!*

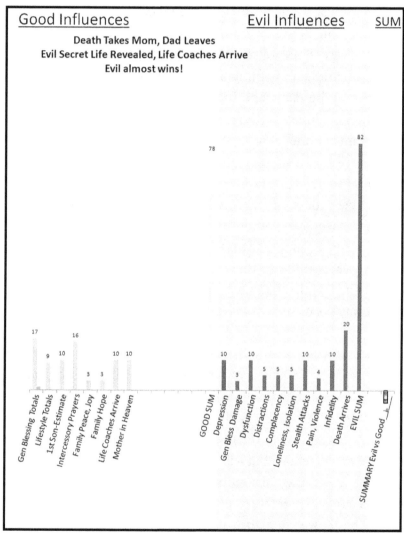

Evil overtakes Good, but the war is not over!

A Hero Arrives

don't remember discipline before I entered Victor Elementary School. Grandpa Lee told the school principal, Mr. Smiley Williams, to discipline me as he saw fit. This instruction came at a time when paddling children was allowed. I can't say I remember him ever paddling me. Instead, the reason I respected him was simply for his style and character of leadership. Either way, he was one of the earliest discipline influences in my life. Many years later, he would return to the crossroads of my life, and his leadership skills would lead me to other happy destinations.

I do now spend a lot of time analyzing the people at the crossroads of my past. I find it useful as a tool for making good decisions about my future. Mr. Smiley would become one of the people who randomly invested in the twists and turns of my life's journey and always did so in a positive way. I know it is true for all of us that if we pay attention to those who wisely led us in the past, it becomes easy to spot good leadership for our future.

Sadly, for too many years that followed, I did not use this wisdom when I made decisions. Instead, I often followed the loudest voice or became the most audible voice in the crowd myself. Today, I am sensitive to not being a sheep. Instead, I believe we all must have times when we are the shepherd. Mr. Smiley taught me how leaders do not have to be the loudest voice in the crowd.

There were other times when people influenced my ability to lead like a shepherd, but Mr. Smiley started this process when he put me on the school safety patrol. Our job was to stand at the crossroads near the school and help others walking to school to safely cross the roads. Soon, I was his captain of the school safety patrol. That placed me as the leader of other crossing guards. Putting me in such a role was risky. Mr. Smiley looked past the predictions for my future and saw a different horizon.

As an early coach in my life, Mr. Smiley taught me lessons in leadership it took me years to appreciate. Today, I see safety at life's crossroads as a critical path. I owe this lesson to Mr. Smiley. A prime objective for my writing is to alert others that healthy crossing guards stand ready to coach us all on life's journeys. There are people just like Mr. Smiley planned to guide us all. Start looking closely for your own Mr. Smiley.

Today, I see my leadership role as a school crossroads safety guard as an early indication of my future expectations. I spend a lot of prayer time thinking about "crossroads intercessions" from my past and planning for similar advice to others. My future role as a leader came under attack immediately after my role as a crossing guard started and continues today.

It was no coincidence that loneliness, disruption, uncertainty, and other evil influences wanted to destroy me. Leadership, confidence, and discipline also showed up to counter their influence. The unseen battle for my life was raging!

Each of us can predict some damage to our lives before we see the harm. Depression and destruction are *always* damaging and can be spotted before they attack. At no time can these influences be described as healthy influences. When they appear, always know they are harmful! But also know they can be defeated. The prescription for healing must come from Dr. Jesus Christ.

Forces like peace, joy, love, happiness, and many others are never hostile. Some troops can go either way. Leadership and competition can turn good into bad or bad into good.

Trust takes some serious consideration to evaluate correctly. I learned not to follow the loudest voice in the crowd. Instead, today I research what I hear, especially from elected officials before trusting what they say. Diversion, deception, deceit, and their sibling liar often show up during this study, but once you find peace, trusting its source bears a lot of fruit! What we trust can be either a mistake or blessing. But truth itself is always a Heavenly Agent.

Just be careful with what you trust!

Once you know what can and does work against your good, avoiding the bad becomes easier. If you like to compete, that battle is one you can welcome. Also, note that not a single person is born a loser. We are all winners. Always know that losing past battles can be overcome with the simple step of accepting Jesus Christ as your Savior. See John 3:16, Romans 10:10, and Romans 10:13. Yes, true trust and faith will then come naturally.

What if I am not a leader? I battle with this often. From my early days as the captain of the Victor Elementary School safety patrol until today, I have led others in one way or another, and the same is true for each of us. Some of us will become significant leaders and influence many people. Others will do so by quiet and constant discipline. One of the most influential clients I ever consulted with saw the determination and moral fiber our staff strives to promote and made a significant change in how he led the political world he influenced. Our quiet and gentle but steady commitment was the catalyst that caused him to revisit his principles.

In our family business, my son Anthony teaches our employees every day. He did not go to a leadership school, but he is very good at leading by constant example. My daughter Melanie taught middle school for years and was a high school coach before joining our family business. She, too, has the leadership skill of being constant and steady. My wife Kim never thought she would be a leader but is the head of business decisions. We all lead, and this includes *you*.

What drives me to write this part of my story is knowing my words will impact at least one soul who needs help. In small or large ways, we can all affect others. We don't all have to be as forceful as I am. Slow and steady is a more common flow. Either way, we should be aware how someone in our path may need our help. And don't forget your prayers can also positively impact generations of your descendants! You can start generational blessings!

Prayers are a powerful tool, but your helping hand is also an expected delivery tool for others. The need for your help may be very close and easy to spot. Other times, we pass by someone in need but never slow down to respond. Your outstretched hand can change the course someone is on with just a tiny touch. Be on the lookout for times when you can be a crossing guide.

Today, as I write these thoughts, I remain heavily burdened over a missed opportunity. While on a consulting job, Kim, granddaughter Zoie, and I landed in Las Vegas and spent the night there before traveling on to our job site.

Together we walked the streets of Las Vegas. We passed far too many who had become homeless. Others wandered the streets with burdens of addictions. Yes, on occasion, the Holy Spirit uses my hand to reach out to some, but I did not feel this influence. Near the end of several hours of walking, I passed a young girl sitting on the sidewalk wrapped in a blanket (it was a rare cold night in Vegas). I noticed a tear in the corner of her eye. She was not begging. Instead, she was just sad. Zoie had never been to a place like this. Her heart was troubled over what she saw. Her compassion for the burdened already existed, but Vegas was her first introduction to the homeless living on the streets.

I led my wife and Zoie to walk past her and into our hotel. I never stopped to see what her burden was. I have stressed over that mistake ever since. Was she in need? Was she even human? Instead, could she have been an angel that was there for me to teach Zoie about mercy? I blew it, and I can't go back and fix it.

Since my story tells of intercessions where I had Heavenly Angels deliver intercession for me in person, I had prayed I could one day see and recognize one before they were gone. Was that young girl the answer to that prayer? How could I fail so badly?

The job I was on the following day was where a very wealthy lady had recently lost much. Her reaction was troublesome, and I was in her presence. I suspect the young girl on the street and this lady had a shared connection. Was I to extend my hand to either of them? Was I to be a crossing guide? Sadly, I stumbled past both opportunities. Forgive me, Lord!

Today, I share the names of but a few of the leaders in my life who impacted me. Influencers like Mr. Smiley led without being called to do so. They did so because of those who taught them to lead by example. I learned about how to reach out through them. I have no excuses for missed opportunities. I know how to guide from the very influencers who impacted my life.

I Am Ruled as Learning Impaired

Before my fourth grade year at Victor Elementary School, I was sent for testing to diagnose why I could not learn and why I was disruptive. Those experts concluded I would never learn like other children and needed special attention and supervision. Sending me away to a place more capable of handling me for the rest of my life was suggested and discussed.

Putting me into a home would have kept me from sharing this story for sure, but that war plan would not be a victory. Mr. Smiley debated this diagnosis and suggested my learning ability was related more to emotional and social reasons than my intelligence. He and my grandparents agreed. This victory is an indication there is always hope for the hopeless.

Mrs. Harper was my third-grade and fourth-grade teacher. I suspect she invested in me so well that she and Mr. Smiley decided to move her and me from the third grade to the fourth grade together. My fifth-grade teacher was Mrs. Margaret Bull, who also owned the community's public swimming pool called Chick Springs. Mrs. Bull's investment took on a healthy character both in and out of school. It was at Chick Springs where I began to be more socially acceptable. Mrs. Bull's leadership also impacted my battle with loneliness.

Chick Springs Swimming Lake

It was many years later when I would learn of Mr. Smiley's investments in my life. He and my grandparents never discussed it, but it is clear today how much he impacted my life, and he did so without praise. I was able to thank him many years later.

In my sixth-grade year, my teacher was Mrs. Harrington. She took her investment in me to a new level. She often invited me and a few other troubled youths to swim and even spend weekends at her home. The learning that started with Mrs. Harper continued through Mrs. Bull and Mrs. Harrington.

Recently, I searched for the descendants of Mrs. Harper and Mrs. Bull. I never found any for Mrs. Harper, but just across the road from my home lived a descendant of Mrs. Bull's family! And yes, he has her strength of character.

It took significant patience and years of extra efforts, but their impact seeded things inside me I so desperately needed. My words about generational blessings continued through each of their families. I know this because I later knew Mrs. Harrington's children, and they also had her strength of character.

Everything, and I do mean everything, can show the hand of our Lord. Mickey Bull's home being across from my home today illustrates how what we may consider a coincidence is the waving of our Lord's hand. His presence is always near!

I struggled all through the years at Victor Elementary. In my last year there, Mrs. Harrington took a switch-blade knife from me just before I could use it on another boy. She did not report this incident. She rescued another boy and me both that day! I had already become violent, and this Evil would grow in me for far too long. Somehow, Mrs. Harrington saw something good in me I did not see myself for years.

Mrs. Harrington's 1965–1966 sixth-grade class.
I am in the back row, second from right.

Mr. Smiley never spoke of these years, but today, I know he invested time in me and others like me. I also know the teachers in front of us truly cared. Today, teachers like him have other names, but they continue to volunteer to be significant influencers in the lives of their students. Sadly though, they are becoming hand-cuffed by other school leaders who are falling victims to the attacks of the evil one. The passion my teachers had is now frowned upon by not all but some public school leaders. We are becoming afraid to be bold, and Evil grows accordingly!

In recapping my days in the elementary school system, I see many sent to my crossroads to guide me on the right path to follow. Some were asked. Others already had the character to lead wisely and volunteered without being asked. We are all a product of those around us and the places we choose to go. Childhood is a short season. Leaders like these teachers are vitally important on this journey.

Today, I imagine some planning for me and others like me was done regularly by teachers and leaders. Somehow, someway, my two children adopted this inherent trait. A desire to coach can be and should be passed down to our descendants. This desire may also come to us from our ancestors' prayers. My children Anthony and Melanie, and my wife, Kim, have this character naturally. They all now coach on numerous levels. Today they all coach and lead others in numerous ways..

Melanie, Kim, Tony, and Anthony Stewart

What a blessing they are in my life and the lives of others. I am blessed to say their strength of character continues in my grandchildren, Colin, Jewel, Zoie, and Emma. This intercession may have begun through my mother's prayers on her deathbed and earlier through my ancestors. Happily, it continues through those nearest to me today. Thank you, Jesus!

Although a study of past mistakes is not the best way to plan a blessed future, it was the catalyst that opened my eyes to how the generational curse can be broken. I now have a passion for teaching this lesson.

One day while saved but living in and choosing to live in sin, I looked down on my young children playing and my wife working too hard to put up with my evil ways and realized I did not want them to follow in my curse. One day, Evil Me also realized I could not lead them wisely. That day, intercessory prayers for me and mine reached a climax in my soul!

Generational blessings can start with any of us. More importantly, anyone not born into a generational blessing can be granted such when they accept Jesus. At that point, generational curses are overturned. This curse was broken for me and can be for you or someone in your heart.

Generational curses are discussed in the Word of God but are often overlooked. You find this in Exodus 20:3–6. These scriptures list God's first commandments where he outlines his expectations for a relationship with him. We focus on the "Thou shalt have no other God" or the "You shall not bow down to other gods." Often overlooked are the results of not keeping these expectations, as seen in verse 5. He mentions he is a jealous God. He then speaks of punishing the children for the sins of the parents for three or four generations! Generational curses are real.

Look at it this way. Bad parenting itself poisons the lives of the children. Learning the character of God the Creator will reveal he does not deliver the punishment. Instead, we as parents curse our children. Realizing this caused me to look into my children's faces and become scared they would follow me. Sadly, such curses can and do last for many following generations.

Additionally, read verse 6. God mentions his rewards, showing love to a thousand generations to those who love and keep his commandments. Don't overcomplicate this important rule. Claim Jesus his son as your Savior, and the curse is broken. Jesus offers the way, the truth, and the light of understanding. God is making it clear that what rules your life should be God. Choose him, accept Jesus, and the curse is broken for you and your children.

Generational blessings can then be delivered to thousands of years of your descendants. Powerful!

Enemies and Allies Will Always Be Nearby

We can easily predict areas where the Fallen One might attack. Some are easy to predict. The enemy Satan hates joy, peace, hope, and love. There are other battlefronts to be concerned about, but these are prime targets where you can expect severe and frequent attacks. Rest assured the Lord Jesus also sees these attacks and provides life coaches and Heavenly Angels to counter them. Learn to spot Evil, and know that once you do, the hand of our Lord is also at work.

When I wrote these exact words, my oldest granddaughter, Jewel Clare Kittrell, just entered her very first class in her first semester at Clemson University. This day brought us great joy! So, an attack against this joy should have been predictable.

As predicted, the enemy did attack. I find this timing no coincidence. Instead, it is proof that comes after faith. The hand of my Lord is everywhere, and occasionally he lets us see it. That morning on June 28, 2021, at 8:00 am, I gave thanks and praise for a wave of his hand when Jewel Clare was in front of new life coaches, such as the leaders and teachers at Clemson University. Students can also be life coaches, sometimes without even knowing it. Early in Jewel's time at Clemson, Izzy and Grace have both impacted Jewel in healthy ways. More will surely follow.

Immediately as I completed the words above about Jewel's first day at Clemson, an interruption came in through an unlikely source, Jewel's mother Melanie, when she asked to store something inside our garage.

My wife Kim and I dropped what we were doing and rushed to arrange a place. A minor disagreement over how best to rearrange quickly attacked our joy. However, this attack was short, and it failed. Not only did I get back to writing, but I was also able to make a new point about this attack against our moments of joy. The happiness over Jewel's first day at Clemson annoyed the evil master. He attacked it by using distraction, which never sleeps!

As soon as I got back to writing, a work-related call came in. I was tempted with some financial gain if I would just drop what I was doing and immediately get busy pursuing it. Distraction is very persistent! Recognizing it in real-time is key to moving past its delays to get back on our course toward joy. As you know by now, distraction may be one of the most persistent Fallen Angels.

Before I began to return to write these words, another distraction arrived. I heard a crash outside and looked out the window and saw a motorcycle accident. The fixer personality took over, and away I went. I rushed out to see if I could be of help. The victim had lost control and laid the bike down. He had some nasty road rash, but his helmet took the worst of the damage. He had just bought the motorcycle that morning and was not yet skilled at driving one.

While waiting for the ambulance to arrive, I was able to keep him from going into shock and used comforting words to give him as much peace as possible. My words eventually calmed him when I showed him the road scars on his helmet. He could then get past the loss of his motorcycle and concentrate on how close he came to having those scars on his face or even ending his life. Peace and comfort can arrive at the crossroads of terrible loss and injury.

I am convinced the enemy used this inexperience to attack my joy and his health and life!

I offer this third distraction to strongly emphasize how the content of what I am currently writing is under severe attack. So, I will not stop until I have made the points that came under attack by distraction, injury, and near death. During this last interruption, I was able to promote peace to an injured man. Distraction lost this battle. Peace arrived and defeated it. What the evil one meant for harm, our Lord turned to his purpose yet again, but distraction will be back!

Life Coach Chip Sloan

Upon entering middle school, I met another powerful influencer who would impact my life for many years to come. Mr. Chip Sloan was in his first year as a gym teacher at Davenport Junior High School and would quickly become my coach in more ways than just sports.

1957: Mr. Chip Sloan

Mr. Chip was next in the long line of people who would introduce me to the real normal. He and my earlier teachers took me well past normal and into blessed and protected territories. Before good men like Chip and Mr. Smiley, evil men had locked me out in the cold while they did unspeakable things with my mother or let me inside to watch or participate. Until these new men taught me otherwise, I believed such behavior was normal. Prior dysfunction lost many battles in my life through the influence of these leaders!

Immediately upon moving in with my grandparents, I began to attend Victor Methodist Church. While it would be years before I accepted Jesus, I did learn some discipline, respect, and accountability. However, it took the loss of many battles before I would use those traits wisely.

Years later, it finally dawned on me that Grandpa Lee and Mr. Smiley created a plan to coach my teachers into providing me with "special treatment." With the diagnosis I could never learn like other children and would be incapable of living a life as an adult without intense supervision, my team of educators had a tough road to travel. Regardless, they chose to hold my future in their hands.

I did not know Mr. Chip was from the same community and home church as Mr. Smiley, Mt. Lebanon Baptist in Greer. Had Mr. Smiley made a call to recruit Chip for me as I entered junior high school? I think not. Instead, Chip and others with the same type of character have chosen to stand at the crossroads of the people they encounter in life.

Mr. Chip would teach me more about staying in shape than I could ever learn in the gym. He was an honest man of both solid character and physical strength. I did not know it then, but Mr. Chip would stand firmly in the crossroads of my life for many years to come. Throughout the years, I have continued to count on his guidance.

In 1981, I was already married to Kim, and we had started our family with our two exceptional children. One cold January night just after Christmas, disaster and death came to our home with a plan to kill us all and destroy our home.

An explosion in our oil-fired furnace erupted into a fire that quickly burned our mobile home to the ground. While we survived, we lost everything, and we had no insurance to replace our home or possessions. Disaster hates joy and especially hates the joy of Christmas. That night, Evil came against our family with an all-out attack.

The Mount Lebanon Church Community and our relatives showed up in force. Chip Sloan's mother, Mrs. Georgia Sloan (who I had never met), offered us her original home place if we would move it to our lot. She asked for less than the cost it took to move it. This house became our first real home and still is to this day.

Mrs. Georgia Sloan

Why these kind people treated us so nicely stuck with me. They knew of my horrible reputation, but they helped anyway.

What Evil meant for bad, Good countered by sending us far more than we lost. We also gained a new family at Mt. Lebanon Baptist Church, which has provided more blessings than could ever be written in words. The disaster that introduced us was no victory against our family. It took a fire that wiped us out to get my attention. The humbleness I desperately needed had arrived, and I noticed him. While not a deathbed experience, the fire was a "near-miss" experience.

There would be many blessings to come in this place. Life coaches like Chip Sloan are in abundance. The same is true for similar churches near you. Mt. Lebanon would also become where many of our family would choose Jesus and be baptized.

In addition, many new life skills are learned in such places. Granddaughters Jewel, Zoie, and Emma met the Lord there. They also learned valuable life lessons led by people like Pam Fowler, Alvin Baker, and many more. They learned team sports, to act, and to sing. They have used such skills to better navigate the roads they will follow throughout their lives. Generational blessings blossom in God's houses.

Destiny works in some unexpected ways. With all the time Chip had spent leading me, I had the blessing to know and mentor his son Andy years later. Then a woman who knew of my then-current choice of an evil lifestyle (Chip's mother Georgia) would bless me with a home. Events such as these are predestined to come. We need to be patient and watch for such intercessions. The long and sometimes twisted roads we travel often take turns that bring about opportunities to touch the lives of others. The leaders at Mt. Lebanon Baptist Church certainly impacted our family.

Our home then and now

We often miss such intercession because the Fallen One works to distract us from seeing this vital resource. The great liar Satan also works overtime to lie to us about church families. He uses the word hypocrite often. There are no forces of heaven named hypocrite. Instead, that is the name of a Fallen Angel! Yes, churches have sinners inside, but Jesus is also there with a promise of forgiveness.

When I finally visited Mt. Lebanon Baptist Church, imagine my surprise when I entered those doors and saw Mr. Smiley Williams and Mr. Chip Sloan again. This was no coincidence. It was part of the long-range battle plan for my life. This church family became my extended family and still is today. Today, the guards at the gates to my family's lives are numerous and robust and filled with our family at MLBC, and these two men are still guiding me. Mr.

Smiley has passed on, but what he taught me lives on through my descendants and me!

Mr. Smiley Williams, Chip and Margaret Sloan

This part of my life story saw several distractions aimed at stopping me from writing. So, I will point out that if the Fallen One sent so many challenges to divert me away from this point, it must scare him a lot! In summary, surround yourself with a supportive family as we did during our time of crisis in 1981. Becoming a part of such a group can eliminate some wars before they start, and one day, you may intercede for someone the way Mrs. Georgia Sloan did for us.

Now, back to my younger years. Even with the investments in my future, there remained many harmful influences like loneliness that were still ingrained in my being. Before and during the powerful influence of these good people, I remained a loner. I did not play well with other children, and my imagination ruled my mind. Creativity can be tricky. It can also be used as a distraction to divert our attention away from good things.

I remember little of any actual class topics during my years at Victor Elementary. I remember sitting at my third-grade desk and drawing forts and underground bunkers instead of writing in cursive. Fear was making its appearance in my life.

The Cuban Missile Crisis was happening at that time, and the fear of a nuclear war saw the building of many underground bunkers in the backyards of homes. Could this have been the Agent of Fear that caused my drawings? Fear desires to dwell with each of us. For me, the third grade was when it made entry into my life. History illustrates how fear also invites violence.

The enemy is always looking for ways to enter our lives and set up permanent influences. Be on guard for even the most subtle and seemingly harmless entry points! Were the drawings of forts and bunkers an invasion point against my future? I do not draw or focus on such things today. Instead, I have peace.

I believe my teachers became alarmed at my drawings, which contributed to my learning impaired diagnosis, and maybe this fueled the advice to commit me to a home for the rest of my life.

Was this the first wave of yet another plan against me? Undoubtedly, yes! Why? Could it have been a part of the plan to stop me from writing these words of truth? Yes, but before we rule this as a new invasion, let me remind you of the knife the man gave me a few years earlier. That knife opened a door of horror into my memory. Was that knife a switch-blade? Did it travel with me through the doors at Victor Elementary School? Indeed, it was and did.

While I would not honor the Fallen One with a label of patience, I will describe his tactics as persistent! I caution that he often works his plans over years. He is proficient at slow-playing his Evil!

About this same time, a new enemy arrived to take up residence in my life. Silently, secretly, fear had come to visit. This Evil is among those whose damage is especially long-lasting. It is so stealthy that only recently did I realize why I was making those drawings. Fear and I became companions. For far too long, fear was my closest friend. Fear never likes it when we make new friends, and hates it when groups of friends spend peaceful time together. It does, however, work well alongside its ally lonely. They are frequent companions.

I quickly became a loner. Making friends at school was not easy for me, and I did not play well at recess. Fighting was common. Primarily, I struggled with teamwork. Fear became the door violence would use to enter my life. Together they pushed away most of my early friends. It was also the goal of fear and lonely that I never play any sports, but this plan would not last long enough to see a complete victory.

Was it time I should be committed to a permanent home and removed from other children? Was this the plan of the enemy? Was he afraid one day my words would reduce his damage to others? What do you think?

The unseen war against me was in full force, but few saw it as a war at all.

As soon as I moved in with my grandparents, I became involved in sports. Grandpa Lee saw to that. By the time Mr. Chip Sloan came along, I had already excelled at baseball, football, and basketball in the youth leagues. Fear hung around a while longer, but lonely was becoming weaker. Violence, however, was silently waiting for its chance to do the most damage.

Grandpa Lee had coached baseball in the textile leagues. The textile teams formed by the abundance of cotton mills in the area and years earlier had included such players as Shoeless Joe Jackson, whose home was in the nearby city of Greenville.

During my years with Grandpa Lee, the textile leagues had evolved into youth programs. He started me off with baseball as my first team sport, and I played for the Victor Mill youth team.

It was the same cotton mill Shoeless Joe played for in 1907 before turning pro in 1908.

Soon there was a list of men who positively coached my over-active energy into focused, productive athletics. With the leadership of men like Robert Gillespie, Ray Vaughn, Billy White, Butch Miller, Riley Jones, and Steve Gambrell, my excess energy took me to all-star levels in every league and sport I played in. Many years later, I would use these skills again to open some very productive doors. This was when I also learned teamwork. My days as a loner were evolving into that of a teammate, but even this strength was feared by the enemy.

Coach Riley Jones and his "Twins" Team

Competition can certainly be a good thing, but it takes a balance I did not always use wisely. However, with the help of crossing guards like the men and women who showed up at significant times in my life, I would eventually learn to channel competition into a healthy thing.

Grandpa knew sports well. His coaching was constant and filled with patience. He also led me into leadership and devotion to our country. He took me to many ball games, some of which were at the American Legion baseball field near our home. Those ball games brought me great joy and also introduced me to patriotic leadership. Grandfather asked if I could raise the American flag during each game-opening ceremony at the legion field.

This dedication to our flag proved helpful as a tool to later spur my interest in serving my country. As small as it may seem, raising the flag gave me a chance to lead others again. Small doors often lead to big rooms.

Grandpa Lee, Mr. Smiley, my teachers, and the folks at the American Legion ballpark saw past my diagnosis of a learning-impaired life. As unlikely as the predictions for me were, I was a leader.

They recognized my unrealized potential. *You can always measure the trueness of your course in life by the amount of opposition to the journey.* The same is true for anyone, and these influencers in my life knew this principle well.

Things are looking up!

Don't Live in the Past

At age nine, when putting me into a home for the rest of my life was discussed, I was certainly no brainiac. Chaos was my constant companion. I was confused, distracted, and hurting, causing the experts to misinterpret all this as a permanent situation.

Today, I make good decisions much of the time but still fall victim to making mistakes, but my past mistakes do not have to be permanent memories. They can be forgiven by simply asking.

If you took my advice and have begun reading the Word of God, perhaps you have read how Jesus said he removes our sins as far as the East is from the West (Ps. 103:11–12). The East never touches the West, and that's powerful. It means he forgets our mistakes and sins! So why do we cling to our past mistakes if he is willing to forget them?

Think about this for a moment. If Jesus forgets them, but we do not, then that's just plain dumb on our part! Why would we want to cling to the mistakes we made when our Creator forgets them? Too many of us let yesterday influence our decisions for tomorrow. That's the wrong way to proceed.

Yes, I tell many stories of yesterday, but I do so as stories of victory.

If yesterday qualifies us to carry its miseries into tomorrow, my past qualifies for millions of years of future pain! We can't work our way to acceptance from God by being a better or wiser person (Eph. 2:8–9) because we will never qualify! All we need to do is believe in Jesus and ask for forgiveness. No amount of mistakes keeps us from heaven after we accept Christ, and no good deeds qualify us to enter his kingdom—faith in Jesus is the only way.

We will all continue to make dumb decisions and commit sins, but once we become children of Christ, then sins can be forgiven. The side benefit of this faithful action is that we learn to make better decisions and more easily spot bad ones! Somewhere in the early years of my mother and father's life, they discovered this simple truth.

Mother knew Jesus before she entered her deathbed. She was able to ask for the forgiveness Jesus had already paid for with his death. In my father's case, many years later and while he lived in my home, I was present when he accepted the Lord Jesus. Today, both of them await our families on the streets of glory!

Living in the past is a distraction that prevents us from seeing the possibilities of our future.

It is imperative to state that living in the past is a curse. When I am asked for a summary of mistakes I see in the lives of people I meet, I mention how holding onto the symptoms of yesterday's mistakes is no way to remove the causes. A bright future is possible, but too many are fooled into thinking a sinful past disqualifies them.

I tell of the war waged against me in my past, but I only do so to promote hope for your future. Once I meet my Savior Jesus in heaven, yesterday's pain will no longer be remembered, and I will be a new man!

Letting the evil one defeat you with yesterday's mistakes is unnecessary. Forgiveness can erase those horrors and bring peace for your future. Distraction works to never let you realize this. Never think you are destined for hell. This falsehood is not true and one of the most damaging lies that Satan tells. *No matter how far you have fallen, a way back to eternal peace will always exist, and that path is through Jesus Christ!*

Is there a way to spot healthy crossing guards? Sometimes looking back can be of benefit. Just note that prevention is a more brilliant way to avoid mistakes. Still, a desire to not make a mistake a second time makes analyzing a previous mistake a resource.

We don't have to look back constantly. There is a resource that helped me to make good decisions in real-time. That helper is called the Holy Spirit, who often guides those who offer us their advice. He is also ever-present in our lives and whispers much wisdom. His guidance is a primary reason that distractions, confusion, related noise, and clutter attack us.

The removal of the healthy guides who will stand diligently at our future crossroads is a primary goal of the Fallen One. I can also tell stories of my past when people blessed me with their friendship and trusted advice. For those friends in my life, it was not always easy or safe to offer to stand on the brink of my crossroads decisions and provide good advice.

Thankfully, healthy guides know of the danger but choose to stand watch anyway. These brave souls are not afraid because the armor of God covers them (Eph. 6:10–18).

Also, standing nearby in each of our decisions is the opposing force against us. Don't blindly follow others down roads without first evaluating the final destination. Think of each travel destination as if you had to look at a map to find your way. Look at the final destination before your trip begins. Know of each turn and where it leads. Today, GPS technology has changed our world substantially, and in my travels, I trust this resource myself. However, I start each journey by looking at a map on my computer and then analyzing each route and alternate routes. I do not trust my GPS to take me to my desired destination blindly, and I certainly do not trust my GPS to take me on a trip to a place I have not researched before I put my hand on the steering wheel!

To enhance your chances of meeting healthy crossing guards, frequent healthy places. It would help if you also guarded your choice of friends. Do some research before inviting people into your life. Look for things that could signal future problems. Look for invisible signs from our Lord. Listen quietly to the voice of the Holy Spirit.

In my case, I learned of the healthy crossing guides in my life by looking backward far too often. Today, I read the Word of God almost every day, over and over and over. Each time, I grow stronger. Each time, I learn more about how our Lord desires to love us. With his love comes the protection we need. With such study comes wisdom to make better decisions. Accordingly, I use this, the Holy Spirit, and prayer to lead me into each journey. With these practices, I can spot life's *Trouble Traps* much easier!

In real-time, let me advise how Evil is often noisy and bright or in your face. Peace is often quiet but steady. Slow down or stop before you go through crossroads and do some peaceful study. Look for the premature gloating of Evil. Listen for the noise intended to drown out your ability to hear from peace. Also, evaluate who your travel companions are and who sent you on this journey. Poor crossing guides are easier to spot when you use these practices.

Use an anointed GPS (God's Positioning System). Our Creator has offered a resource we often overlook. He has sent his Holy Spirit to guide us. His Holy Spirit is always with those who are children of his Son Jesus. The Holy Spirit is also within reach of those who do not claim Jesus. This resource is a part of the Trinity—Father, Son, and Holy Ghost. Why not look for his guidance at each of the twists and turns in your road through life?

Even if you are not yet a believer in Jesus Christ, what have you got to lose by reading his Book every day and seeking advice from the Holy Spirit? Indeed, read the Bible just before you make a significant decision on an upcoming turn in your life. You may just find the answer you need.

The ability to fully understand and use his words must come through the Holy Spirit. Without that, it is only a book made of leather, paper, and ink. Without the Holy Spirit, understanding truth is almost impossible. Without the guidance of the Holy Spirit, the evil liar convinces you errors exist.

Every trade school, every college promotes study materials for gaining knowledge of your future career. Devote yourself to reading God's Word and visiting the places he calls his house. Surrounding yourself with this kind of environment will work to reduce taking wrong and blind turns. Then you will start seeing his Holy Spirit posting signs at each of your crossroads decisions. I don't mean a visual warning. Instead, a wave of his invisible hand can and will use earthly things to point the way.

Here are but a couple of examples of how he counsels. Both of these stories saved lives. One is mine, and the other is from the lives of two little old ladies.

One busy day, I was in a rush to get to a job site. On my drive, I was on a six-lane highway and fell in behind a tractor-trailer that was not moving as fast as I wanted to go. My immediate plan was to pass him. However, I also felt I should have a little patience and follow behind him. Next, I realized I would soon merge onto the interstate highway and decided I did not want to stay behind this truck if he would merge ahead of me.

I decided to pass him, and there were two available lanes on our side of the road, so I was about to change lanes and jump in front of this truck. Then my thoughts changed back to being patient. I again decided not to change lanes to get in front of him. A battle for my life was underway. The Holy Spirit told me to be patient. I obeyed. The suggestion of being patient was very brief.

In just a few seconds and while I was still behind the big rig (and following too closely), just as we approached the ramp to the Greenville Spartanburg International Airport (on our left), I noticed motion. I looked that way to see an airplane crashing to the ground.

This small airplane had run out of fuel while approaching the landing strip, then hit the guardrail just in front of the big truck missing him by very few feet, traveled across the road at almost road height, hit the other side guardrail, and then crashed just short of the runway.

Had I passed this truck, I would have been in front of the truck right where the plane traveled after hitting the first guard rail. I would have been on the news as the person killed by a plane hitting my car. The Holy Spirit works to guard and save us from tragedy. Patience fought rush and won. My life was spared, and death was also defeated. The Holy Spirit orchestrated this rescue with one voice heard inside my head: patience!

Let me offer another example even while realizing there are many others rescues sent my way I never knew about. With some practice and the guidance of the Holy Spirit, you will notice similar events in your life. Another day while traveling and in another rush, I sat at a red light behind two little old ladies. The ladies were talking and not looking at the light. When the light turned green, they did not drive through the light. Instantly, I was ready to blow my horn, but patience spoke up and said not to.

Next, a fully loaded dump truck ran its red light! Had I impatiently honked my horn, would they have pushed the gas pedal and been hit broadside by the dump truck? Rush again had invited death to kill those two ladies. The Holy Spirit used patience to defeat the plan. Listen for patience (John 14:26; Acts 2:38; Isa. 11:2). It is a gentle voice and often overlooked. Yes, the Holy Spirit speaks the wisdom of our creator God to sinners too!

I hope those little ladies and I will meet one day where traffic lights don't exist.

Rush and hurry have claimed the lives of too many. Cell phones have been deadly tools they use. Haste and impatience join in the battle strategy to invite death and injury to impact lives.

Evil smiles at each loss.

How do you spot healthy crossroads guides? My best advice is to invite the Holy Spirit to guide you. Can you do this if not a believer in Jesus? Well, the Holy Spirit is free to act for each of us. Just don't count on him accompanying you into places of Evil or when you are doing Evil yourself. Once a child of the Risen King Jesus, the Holy Spirit is always beside you (Luke 1:67; 11:13; Matt. 3:11). Yes, he was near me before I was a Christian, but I pushed him away or ignored him! How about you?

If you are not yet a Christian, then at the very least start looking and listening for the Holy Spirit at your next crossroads.

Since 1993, I have been in the smart house industry. I have met and solved technical problems for many of the world's wealthy and famous people. Each time, I start my day onsite by leading the other contractors and homeowners in prayer. More than once, a prosperous soul would choose to debate my beliefs. My intercessory prayer for him or her asks that something extraordinary enter his or her life and becomes known to him or her from where it came.

This kind of righteous prayer is often answered. Why? Because our Lord desires to make himself known, but more so because he loves to answer such prayers for us. How he does it is not always known to me. What I do know is that a blessing comes to them, and its origin often becomes apparent. What they do with this, I never know. However, I think I will one day meet some of them on the streets of glory and find out!

Sometimes my comeback, when they choose to debate, is to suggest they do a thorough study of the Word of God and share with me their thoughts and concerns. Opinions often changed for those who studied with the same discipline they used to learn the skills required for their professions. I am not saying proof exists. Instead, faith is the only way to an accurate understanding. I am saying that some of my clients became lifelong believers soon after they were brave enough to seek. The rewards for this decision are countless. You can quickly count on one of these rewards, which is the daily presence and counsel of the Holy Spirit.

Am I saying the day you become a Christian you will instantly experience such miracles? Maybe. Most of the time, though, they will not be noticeable. Many rescues came in ways I never realized. The same is true for all of us.

By the way, since time does not exist in heaven and there are certainly no alarm clocks, rush and haste will never be a thought we will have there. Another vital point to make is that rush and peace do not exist simultaneously or in the same place.

Finding Peace in Unlikely Places

Peace is possible even in unlikely places and situations. To keep us from realizing a battle against our future is being waged, another plan to cause us to miss blessings is also underway.

Here is a good example. As I write this chapter, I am in Scottsdale, Arizona, consulting on installing electronics in a large commercial facility under construction. My role will be to select all the electronics, design the system, and guide the installation of all subsystems, including the fire alarm system. I planned to wake up on Eastern time each morning and use the three-hour time difference to write this chapter. However, I traveled with a sciatic nerve issue, making walking painful. During physical pain, it is customary not to have the best focus, but I am determined to write this morning.

At 3:30 am Pacific time, I woke up in my hotel room and immediately thought about writing. I find early mornings are a time of clarity for me. I have had some tremendous early morning talks with the Lord, and I am counting on that this morning.

Three minutes later, the hotel's fire alarm goes off. Fire trucks arrive, and eventually the false alarm is silenced. Writing about how to find peace requires a time of peace. My body is in pain; I am annoyed over the noise from the fire alarm; I have lost sleep, and the hotel staff did not handle the alarm quickly enough.

After this, I have no peace of mind, and I wrestle with myself over not writing anything, but I start again. I eventually find my peace and begin to write. Soon, I hear strange scratching noises above my room's ceiling. Again I am annoyed, and peace is lost.

My plans have now changed to focus on the complaints I will make to the hotel's management later this morning. I plot to introduce myself as an expert on fire alarm systems and complain about noises above my ceiling.

Distraction is doing a victory dance nearby. Peace is under attack!

As dawn comes and I try to write again, I lack peace. As a result, I go back and delete my words. Something important that should be said in this chapter is now lost in the clutter of noise.

When the sun makes its daily appearance, young birds in the nest always begin their calling for food. The scratchy sounds above my ceiling change to the calls of these birds asking for their morning feeding. I now plan to raise the blood pressure of hotel management to complain there are birds roosting above my single-story room. Peace falls further down on my list of priorities, and the words of peace and hope I should have been writing are no longer a priority. Distraction is a known enemy to writers, but I did not expect it to introduce the Evil of complaining into this battle.

Then I hear a small quiet voice in my head say, "Grab your laptop, a cup of coffee, and go out on the patio of your room to watch the sun come up," and I obey. Immediately the peace of morning arrives. I see mama birds at work gathering the food their children are crying for. Rabbits navigate up to almost within my touch. Peace has come, and nature ushered it in. The sounds of birds fill the air. Relaxation has now welcomed peace to return. Ten feet away from my early morning misery is peace. I now wonder if our Lord's soldiers of peace could appear as birds and rabbits. They can, but this morning, peace came from a creation that has been around since the dawn of time—nature itself! Finally, here is what I was supposed to write!

The small voice I heard in my head didn't mean I was crazy. That voice was the counsel from the Holy Spirit. That voice and nature are both messengers of peace this morning. Slow down and pray, and you, too, can see past distractions intended to rob you.

The pool guy is working, the air is clear, and a new day has begun. I will not tell management about the bird's nest. I will likely offer some fire alarm system advice to help solve the problem, but I will not criticize the night manager's actions. Later, I decide against even doing that. It takes some searching, but I find some kind words to share with management instead.

I was about to miss writing this example entirely. As an opinionated and prideful big-shot national expert on fire alarms, I was about to hurt the night manager's career and influence the killing of some baby birds. Of course, the analysis of this distraction would not have been possible. Thank you, Lord, for once again showing me your hand.

Later, I met two men who traveled with me to this location, Rogelio Zuniga and Bruce Redmon. They had slept through the fire alarm! I can only assume this lesson was for me alone.

Let me share my last thought before I begin my day in the lovely state of Arizona.

Instead of asking for a new room, I will not. Instead, I will put up with false alarms and birds above my ceiling for the next three nights of my visit. If the Fallen One went to so much trouble to rob my readers of this example of peace, then I know I am right where I am supposed to be. I am now looking forward to hearing my early morning bird alarm clocks. I could do without the horns from the fire alarm, but I doubt it will happen because I have seen the hand of the evil one who sent this havoc, and it is doubtful he will use the same diversion again. I will also smile when the pain from my sciatic nerve fills my back and left leg. This type of pain will not distract me again.

Choose Friends Carefully

Spiritual warfare can happen on any battlefront location. Some are easier to predict than others. Why? Because some battle-grounds are easier to gain entry through than others. Where we choose to spend our time can open the door to losses in our lives. The opposite was the case at the home of my grandparents, so a more detailed invasion plan was required.

Rocky and Rob (not their real names) were brothers who often visited our field of play at Grandma's home. Rocky was my age and became a running buddy on our journeys through the mill village neighborhoods near where we lived. They introduced me to a whole new level of violence. They were the ones who intro-duced me to the art of using a knife and gun. Yes, I had just turned fourteen, and yes, Rocky was with me when I tried to use a knife for the first time.

What I learned from their lifestyle would not fully impact me until years later. Eventually, Rocky would die in a gun battle with a Georgia sheriff's deputy, and Rob would spend most of his life in prison for murder. I came close to both of their destinations, but intercession came. More than once, it took the appearance of Heavenly Angels to help me past these *Trouble Traps.*

New and powerful enemies to my future had arrived. They lived just outside the farthest regions of my garden home, but they were close enough to come onto that sacred ground slowly. Strangely, they dared not come close to the house and never entered. Could it have been that the Evil living in them feared approaching the Holy Spirit living in my grandparents? I think so.

There were also healthy spirits that visited. They came inside friends like Chris Dumas, one of those crossroads guides standing guard at some of the most critical decisions in my future. Many years later, Chris would one day open the door to a workplace for me when my young family needed a dependable job the most. Chris stood by me even when my reputation advised otherwise.

Chris and Linda Dumas

In the first year of my marriage to Kim, I was still struggling. There were no good jobs in electronics, and I worked as a furniture manufacturer for a time. It was a back-breaking job that taught me how to work efficiently and diligently.

This job had no benefits, and our son Anthony was on the way. I needed some help. I learned Chris was working at a manufacturing company where I wanted a job in electronics. I called him, and he eagerly shared how I should approach their human resources department.

I called, and in a short time, I was back in the field of electronics and employed as a fixer once again. Chris knew of my past but remembered our earlier friendship. He was a volunteer as a crossroads guide for me once again. Years later, I had a role where Chris became my supervisor. This kind of relationship is ordained. However, you must be willing to listen or become a guide yourself. I listened, and Chris led!

On one front, Rocky and Rob were pulling me into a world of violence. On the other front stood a few like Chris, who would guide me to heavenly places one day. The Fallen Angel, however, had a plan to stop Chris and me completely. He knew this friendship would not work toward his goals of destruction. His assault plan was put into place years before Chris and I would work together. Explosions and death were his chosen soldiers.

It happened just after I got my driver's license. Chris was driving the 1957 Chevrolet my dad had bought me on one of his returns to the USA from Africa. I had purchased over a hundred cherry bombs, and we were going around launching them out of the windows of my Chevy. One cherry bomb could blow off a finger, and we had enough of them to blow up our car and kill us both. That evening, our death was the plan.

I lit one and went to throw it out of my window. Instead of going out of the window, it hit the inside top of the door's window and bounced back inside and onto the dash. All the other cherry bombs were nearby in the front seat. The explosion ruined the windshield but did not land near the rest of the cherry bombs.

The Fallen One, Satan himself, planned to end both of our lives that day. Mighty angels stepped in and pushed that cherry bomb into a small crack on the dash just under the windshield. Had it landed anywhere else, this story would have never been told. This kind of miraculous intercession happens for us all. Learning to see and appreciate it takes some quiet prayer time.

There would be many more such events along my journey to peace and salvation. Most came during the worst and most Evil days of my life. Thank you, Lord, for sparing Chris and me.

Good or bad friends can enter our lives through countless doorways. After my mother died, music became a passion for me and increased my circle of friends substantially. Loneliness was temporarily replaced with busyness. Music eventually invited evil allies to join the invasion team. These allies were popularity, loudness, and flashing lights.

Just after I turned thirteen, my father came home to visit. He bought me an electric guitar. Why? It was because when he visited, he would frequent a local bar. He met a friend there who was a manager of his son's local rock band. Together they formed a plan for me to one day join their band. Eventually, and after a lot of noisy practice in my grandparents' home, I joined this band and learned to love traveling and playing rock-n-roll music. The members of the band had sound characters. I was the misfit. The band included people who had a lot better grasp on a healthy life than I did.

I eventually formed a band of my own. We played at birthday parties, had a few travel dates, and played for Blue Ridge High School events a couple of times. Before I was fifteen, I was a local rock star (or so I thought). What I did not see was how I was being pulled away from my healthy lifestyle. Evil can attack us using success and even popularity. Both of these traits can cloud our ability to recognize Evil's other influences growing nearby.

The skills I learned as a guitarist and a singer seemed innocent but proved otherwise. My choice of friends slowly drifted away from the quality I had when I was a member of the first band I joined and into a circle of friends of a different and more dangerous character.

Even during these years, good crossroads guides were standing nearby. Carol Sims was the daughter of the Greer First Baptist Church pastor. She asked me to attend a revival where he preached. Although not yet a believer, a seed was sown within me. She was also present at some of the performances where my bands played. Friends like Carol and Chris fertilize good choices, and people like them are often standing nearby in our lives, but I had not yet learned to separate good friends from evil influences.

Amazingly, Carol and Chris chose to associate with me. Both had a history of a strong family bond and were wise enough to avoid people like me. It was the hand of our Lord Jesus that influenced them to stand in my crossroads.

I often think of a miracle that occurred at that revival. When it was over, Carol and I walked to my car. I realized I had locked the keys inside. The first man to walk by tried his key, and it worked to open my door! This may seem insignificant, but it was once again the hand of our Lord sending intercession. He works to show his hand in many ways.

It was no coincidence Chris Dumas was also present in my time at Victor Methodist Church and that Carol was with me at my first revival experience. I must also note how Mr. Smiley and Chip Sloan were anchored in what would become my home church at Mt. Lebanon Baptist Church. The hand of our Lord visible at the previous crossroads of our lives will often show up in our future! The man with the key that fit my car probably showed up again somewhere along the way.

Carol Sims Paret

Atlanta is a beautiful place. I can't say enough good things about it. However, every city has a place like the Back Row in Greer, which you'll learn more about shortly. The difference between the two was that the culture in Atlanta, where drugs could be bought, was much older than the one growing in the Back Row in Greer. I would soon fertilize the Back Row drug culture.

During my time as an entertainer, I tried pot. It all started innocently enough when other musicians and I heard we could smoke pot and play music better. This was a lie. Still, we traveled 150 miles to Atlanta to buy some pot from street dealers. We were satisfied with our efforts to purchase. The final result would prove to be a horrible mistake.

As a musician, I made very little money, and pot was not cheap. Soon, the only way to pay for my pot was to buy enough to resell. That was the start of me as a drug dealer. Other users lacked skills in sales and became thieves to fund their habit. A desire to smoke marijuana started innocently enough, but soon after came other drugs.

On another trip to Atlanta, it was suggested we try LSD. We did. I know now how drugs can have Opposing Agents attached to them. Violence is one of them. Poor judgment is another. The Evil named theft took up residence in many users, even users of just pot.

My journey to misery was now following in the footsteps of my mother, and Evil was winning. The Fallen Angel smiled. Soon, a new enemy arrived, whose name was rebellion. It was a different drug on a different street, but the goal to destroy us all was the same.

During the summer when I was fourteen, I hitchhiked to Atlanta without telling anyone I was leaving. The character of the man who picked me up on Interstate 85 that day was a new experience. I had to use my violent skills to fight that man off. The Word of God describes how he feels about people with the character of this man—anger!

Another evil influence was learned on that ride. Its name was perversion. The pervert who gave me a ride left that meeting with a black eye from me. I was left on the side of the road until I could thumb another ride. I made it to Atlanta and slept that first night on the streets.

On the streets, I was befriended by members of a motorcycle gang. I learned much about drug and alcohol use, community sex, and fighting during my time with them. I became much better at being very bad, especially when it came to fighting skills and violence. It was a constant factor with this gang of people, and battles with other gangs happened. Torture, knife, and gun use won victories. I would use those evil skills later and often.

Today, another of my old friends is Ross Burgess. He walked similar roads of danger before coming to the Lord Jesus. Today, he and some of his fellow motorcycle riders spend their time promoting hope to the hopeless. I share his victory story happily, but Ross will agree that most of those we called friends years ago are gone today without ever finding peace. He and his club have a passion for ending this lifestyle of misery by introducing people to Jesus. I join them in their plan to promote hope for the hopeless. Today, they are called Bounty Hunters for Jesus. Ross and his friends are among my heroes, and we need more like them!

Ross Burgess, the Bounty Hunter for Christ!

Years later, in a fight at a concert where I was alone and jumped by some thugs, I would pull a gun, point it at the head of a man from four feet away, and pull the trigger. An intercessory angel intervened, and the bullet hit the road. When I turned to look at this person, he was gone. It would be many years later before I realized this was a Heavenly Angel. Aunt Audrey or Grandmother Blanch Charity had most likely dispatched this angel through intercessory prayer.

You may think some Evils will only happen once. Wrong! Concert fights and barroom brawls would make appearances to me often. For a time, I was lost in the clutter of music, lights, and smoke. During that time, I missed many outstretched hands of hope. They reached out to me, but I slapped them away.

After a few weeks on the streets of Atlanta, I returned to my grandparents' home. Aunt Audrey and others prayed for me. Some of my younger cousins began to have nightmares about me coming to their home and hurting them. Evil won a major victory when I was fourteen. Evil stayed well-hidden as he gloated. I had fully become Evil Me!

How I returned home should be mentioned. One of the more fierce and violent gang members took me under his wing and cared for me. I learned to trust evil leadership. I needed a friend, and he filled that void. After a few weeks on the summer streets of Atlanta, he insisted I get on his bike for a ride home to make sure I went back to school before the summer ended!

Evil hides like this. It can disguise itself in the form of someone acting as if they want to help. People around us often use lies like this. The result is that several people hunker down together and enable each other. Looking back, I see that what I benefited from during my time with him taught me how to hurt myself and others in more harmful ways than I ever knew before.

I wonder what happened to this leader of Evil. I pray he and all others I met along my journeys of Evil found true peace. What are the odds of that? I hope and pray he met someone like Ross Burgess standing in his crossroads, pointing the way to healing, peace, and hope—better yet, to eternal salvation through Christ Jesus.

It's not enough to talk about being near Evil or death and narrowly escaping. We must learn to look deeper, even into the future. The enemy always has other goals that go well past immediate destruction. This master of distraction can somehow predict our future, or he can at least see our potential better than we can. Remember yet again: *We can often measure the trueness of our course in life by the amount of opposition to it by the enemy!*

An example of this was the near-death event with the cherry bombs that would have stopped my friend Chris Dumas from being around to positively affect my life as he was to do years later, assuming I would have lived through the intended accident at all.

Chris would start a family with Miss Linda Wood, and they and their son Lee would impact many others in positive ways. Indeed, they are examples of generational blessings. Death came to rob Chris and me because he feared what would come from us both if he let us alone. He feared our future generations. Chris's descendants, my wife Kim, and our children and grandchildren also play roles in the lives of many, delivering generational blessings, and this greatly bothers the evil one!

Death was an early and frequent visitor to my life. Why did an angel cause me to miss shooting and killing that man in the parking lot of that concert? Intercession was not just for me. The future of others was also included in that intercession.

Could it be the man I almost killed also had an intercessory angel alongside him? I say yes. That intercession was not just mine. Many lives were affected by that intercession. Think about this in the quiet times when you ponder the crossroads experiences of your life, but don't assume intercession will always spare you from harm.

The Back Row Culture

For a time, peace, love, and hope embraced me daily. I had plenty of life coaches, but Evil was not ready to give up on overcoming me with the grief he loves to spread. Subtly, silently, Evil was creeping up for a major surprise attack.

My journey back into misery began with my choice of places, things, and people. Not all at once, but slowly, I took several small steps away from my haven of hope. The pathway was music, then rebellion, and then violence.

This chapter tells of a place and culture that distracted and slowed my journey to peace. A similar plan is in place for all of us. Places and the people we meet at such locations are often used against us. You can count on an abundance of Evil being present at such sites.

I am not proud of this story. I tell it in hopes you can spot such a place and avoid it. If not, count on suffering loss.

Soon after I got my first car, I replaced my haven at my grandparents' home with a spot in what was called the Back Row of a local hang-out spot. I first encountered this place when one of my baseball teammates introduced me to underage drinking, which evolved into pot, then pills, and then anything I could get. I never saw people like Chris or Carol at my new chosen place.

Being a leader has consequences. I loved leading and found my previous expertise with my mother and drugs in such places caused many on the Back Row to seek my counsel. I must have bragged about my horrible past. What a mistake that was! People listened. I led, but this time, my shepherding skills did not help people safely cross the streets.

Ronny was a long-time friend who had never done any drugs. He and I had begun to play some music together. When he approached me on the Back Row with questions, I sold him on the idea drugs were great. I lied, and he died! He did not die at my hands. Instead, I was only one of the lost leaders. I should have led my dear friend to safety. I was not present when it happened. I did not sell or give the drugs to him, but he overdosed and died soon after beginning his journey.

Although I was not his drug dealer, my influence accompanied him to his last breath.

Ronny died that day, but my ability to give bad advice and lead others to destruction only grew. I was no longer the captain of the school crossing guard. I was the captain of evil leadership! My title as Evil Me was entirely earned. In this place we called the Back Row, many others began their journeys to death, and I promoted such a lifestyle. At fifteen years of age, I was a leader of the lost!

I see my ability to be forgiven by our Creator as a blessing, and I will not be depressed over this mistake, but I do long for my time in eternity when no memories of my early burdens or mistakes will exist. When I enter those gates, no thoughts of yesterday's mistakes will follow me. I long to see Ronny there, and I hope I will.

Liar, killer, murderer! All of these influences grew stronger inside me after Ronny's death. The place we chose to hang out became poison, and my friends and I did not know it. Places like the Back Row have evil angels assigned to them. Their jobs are numerous, and all are deadly. After a visit to the Back Row, evil spirits traveled back to my haven with me. I invited them!

During those days, numerous people reached out to me. There were many crossroads guides, life coaches, and leaders reaching out to me. Instead of grasping those helping hands, I violently pushed them away. Violence was the kind of skill I learned on the streets of Atlanta and perfected on the Back Row. The Evils that grew there would also follow me back home and grow in strength.

The plan to gain access to the inside of my grandmother's haven of peace took years, but it found success that day. Other friends and some of the cousins in our family also had fear come into their lives that same way, providing yet more evidence I was indeed Evil Me.

At the crossroads where Evil and I stood together, we chose to join other families of miserable souls who, like us, have a history of defeat. After that, Evil can then loosen its grip on us, knowing our own bad choices will drive us further downward. He also knows that once we join a "back row" culture, those around us will keep us from seeing hope.

Separation flexed its muscles on the Back Row often. Loneliness grew while surrounded by numerous companions. The intercession I was surviving on continued, and the rescue missions continued to be sent. My troubles, however, were not over and had not yet reached their peak. Absolute misery lay just ahead.

My Back Row family grew. More and more people like me joined us. A "party" is what we called our sessions together, but always nearby was a growing army of Evil, an Evil that no longer hid in the shadows; an Evil that boldly claimed its victims, and we all just watched and waited for our turns.

When Ronny died, I would choose the Back Row for a while longer, and the joy I once had moved further away. The light of hope was growing dim.

Soon, I met people who advised me to leave the Back Row and move away from my grandparents' haven of hope. I took a break from this culture to join the Air Force. Just before the evil agent of death came for me, I left the Back Row. My intercessors had never given up on me.

Thank you, Lord, for those crossing guards!

Can We Meet Hope at Our Chosen Places of Misery?

Years later, I would return to my old, evil hunting grounds again. Hanging out in the Back Row did not open the door to finding my soul mate before my time in the Air Force. Instead, it would be years before I would see her, and I found her not in the Back Row but just across the street of the infamous Back Row. The point I make is that somewhere nearby is always a doorway out of misery. It took only a few steps away from the Back Row to find love and peace!

This is the way our Lord works. Please take a few steps toward him and eternal peace can be found. See Romans 3:10, Romans 6:23, and Romans 10:9.

After some time in the USAF, I made the same Back Row mistakes again, and I was more proficient at being bad, especially when it came to violence.

My wife Kim was sent to be near my crossroads. Somehow and during my most blind days, I was able to see something different and wonderful just across the street from my chosen place of Evil!

I advise you to be alert and on the lookout for those Earthly Angels sent to intercede for us. Kim Lemmons was not a prior visitor to the Back Row, but she did show up just outside the gates of this evil place. This was also an answer to prayers of intercession my family offered for me. This chance meeting was ordained and not a coincidence.

Also, know this fact: No matter where we are, hope is nearby. It takes a few steps away from the darkness to find it, but hope is within our reach. The point to strongly consider about our chance meeting is that we don't have to be too far away from our bad place to find hope.

Earthly Angels and people sent to intercede for us often do not know of their role at all. They may be near our misery but will rarely be found in our old haunts. Our Lord does not give up when we do. He is never defeated. Know that somewhere very near your place of defeat is your better future. Whether you pick a horrible place or one filled with hope, there will still be a choice you must make. Clear your thoughts and be on the lookout. Know you must often take a few steps away from Evil to realize your destiny.

High School Influences

Let me backtrack to set this scene. It happened years before I met Kim.

By the time I started the ninth grade at Greer High School, I had abandoned sports and replaced them with hard rock music and drugs. I had replaced healthy friends and life coaches with others who shared the Back Row culture. I was ignoring healthy influences, and my grandparents were too old to control me. Besides that, they used things like love to lead me. Love was not working on me. Thank God for the continued intercessory prayers of Aunt Audrey and the others who never gave up on me.

As I look back on my high school years, I see plenty of people who reached out to me with helping hands, whether by example or by taking an active part in my life. Mrs. Nelly Gordon was the Greer High School nurse. I probably met her because of a lie I told about being sick. Why she would desire to guide me is still a mystery, but she did. I am left to believe she was eager to intercede with anyone. It was in her natural character to do so. She was a fixer! This kind of spirit was present in many who reached out to me. Some I embraced, others I hurt.

On her desk, I spotted a picture of her daughter Mimi. When I asked about her, she invited me to meet her. This had to be an act of compassionate intercession. Through this chance meeting with Mimi, I would eventually enter the Air Force. Our road to healing and hope can take some surprising turns, especially when the Lord Jesus sends agents of mercy like the Gordon family to help.

During my time with the Gordon family, I somehow managed to stay clear of the Back Row culture, but I was not smart enough to embrace Christ yet. The Gordon family, however, sure did.

Didi, Mimi, Nelly, and Gigi Gordon circa 1971

My lifestyle was a wreck, and I needed a way out that did not involve Greer. I was seventeen, failing the eleventh grade, and had no plan for my future. Mrs. Hayes was the guidance counselor at Greer High School, and she and Mrs. Gordon stepped up to offer me a way out.

At Greer High, I had been suspended several times for fighting in school. My reputation was already horrible and permanently damaged. Mrs. Gordon must have known this. Her choosing to help me proved she was a lady of solid Christian character.

Mrs. Hayes asked me to take the South Carolina high school general equivalency test and advised me that with a diploma, I could then enter the military at age seventeen. The Vietnam war was happening, and so was the draft. I liked the idea to get a change of scenery and a chance to fight in Vietnam. I did not expect it to be an answer to intercessory prayers for me.

Mrs. Gordon offered her daughter Mimi as my tutor, and the course was set. Mimi and her sisters Didi and Gigi were descended from generationally blessed parents who also taught them to be fixers. They must have known what a risk I was, but they still volunteered. With Mrs. Gordon opening the door and Mimi leading the way, the course my life would follow began. For a time, Mimi also removed loneliness from my life.

Mimi spent a lot of time mentoring and teaching me. Their attraction to me was in their family strengths. They were contagious. Mimi invested weeks in my training and demonstrated leadership I had seldom seen. She also taught me how I should treat a girlfriend. Mimi and her family positively impacted my life. I am deeply grateful for the Gordon family! They arrived at the crossroads of my life at just the right time. They are on my all-time heroes list. Without their mentoring, I would have never gotten past my troubled years and into the USAF.

Mimi's father was a retired major in the Army, and her mother was an Army nurse. Both also hoped for my future as a serviceman. The world could use more families like theirs. They replaced my family on the Back Row and at precisely the right time. Their military ties and my time in the American Legion park combined to make entering the military a desire for me.

I easily passed the GED test and entered the USAF during Vietnam at age seventeen. Still thinking about violence, after boot camp, I tested for their special forces unit known as Pararescue, referred to as PJ, and immediately went into training. I was finally away from the influences that had won so many victories against me back home, and I was ready to fight!

I was among the youngest PJs ever to be accepted into the program. In my heart, I still harbored violence. I saw being a PJ as a way to exercise it freely. I learned to box and was a lightweight winner at 155 pounds. Everything was set for me to be a killer. I had the desire, physical fitness, training, and opportunity to travel to Vietnam as a PJ and rescue others behind the enemy lines.

I was ready to kill, but the Lord had another plan for me.

During the PJ indoctrination program at Lackland AFB in San Antonio, Texas, we ran from ten to twelve miles a day in cadence, swam many miles, and learned hand-to-hand fighting. We also played tackle football and boxed for fun.

I had no genuine desire to rescue anyone in Vietnam as a PJ. Instead, my real goal was to travel to Vietnam as a finely polished man of violence. Then, during a game of tackle against some Army guys, I was gang tackled. This busted me up pretty badly, but on Monday, it was time to run and train again. Soon I fell to the rear of the pack due to my football injuries, but I was determined to finish my miles. I did finish and never stopped running, although I could not run in cadence with the others and finished much later than they did. I painfully ran my entire twelve miles that day and finished a couple of hours after the others.

I had seen many DORs (Drop out On Request), but I did not DOR. Instead, I was determined to stay and work through this injury and pain. My sergeant felt otherwise. Usually, the quitters got their butts kicked on the way out of the building. In my case, he dropped me, stating my injury would take too long to heal, and a PJ had to have a perfect body. Today, I know the Lord had a different future in mind for me. Had I stayed a PJ, duty in Vietnam was killing many of them. I would likely have been in the gun sights of the devil's sharpshooter.

After some time healing, I was sent to electronics school at Keesler AFB in Biloxi, Mississippi. Today, I know our Lord influenced this decision, and my sergeant was his tool. It is doubtful my injury was the reason. Like the Gordon family and so many others, he was used as an agent of hope for me.

After leaving Pararescue, I felt like I was a failure. I didn't realize how not being a PJ answered intercessory prayers from my family, friends, and probably many ancestors praying for future generations.

My short stint as a PJ once again opened the doors for leadership in the USAF. This doorway was started by my grandfather, Mr. Smiley, many teachers, Chip Sloan, the Gordon family, and others. Real heroes like these never give up on praying for intercession and never let past mistakes label anyone as hopeless.

My Drug Trafficking Sentence

During my time in the USAF and while in electronics school in Biloxi, I became a Christian. This fantastic and miracle-filled story began a journey that needs its own book someday.

With a career as an electronics fixer, I was not sent to Vietnam. Instead, I was sent to Shaw AFB in South Carolina as a radio repairman, and once again, pretty close to a Special Forces unit involved in forward air support. This time, we were based stateside. Life was looking good!

With this assignment, my Biloxi Christian support group was no longer with me. Soon the short two-hour drive from Shaw AFB to my hometown of Greer, South Carolina, opened the door to visits to the Back Row again. Yes, I fell back into misery and Evil again. Only this time, I was much more capable of being violent.

I made the rank of sergeant much faster than most. Maybe it was my history as a PJ that brought me to the head of the promotion list, but I believe my new rank as a leader also answered intercessory requests for me to be a shepherd. I blew that too.

Instead of leading those under me, I used my authority to create more days at home instead of more time on base, giving me more time on the Back Row. Soon I was again selling drugs on the Back Row and ignoring my future in the USAF. Then one day, I sold PCP to an undercover agent. Where? On the Back Row, of course!

Each day on the Back Row, I lived with conviction. I knew Jesus, and I was his child, but I was choosing Evil once again. A deep feeling of being convicted came over me anytime I was sober and not using drugs or alcohol, which was not very often. I am not talking about being convicted of a crime, though that kind of conviction was soon to come as well.

The all-out war against my future had begun its final phase. Time in a military prison followed, then a discharge from the USAF followed, as did time in city and county jails. The city jail time was in the same city where, eighteen years later, I would serve as a police officer with no criminal history—yet another improbable miracle to come my way.

What Evil thought was the last battle against me was not. Instead, I was to one day write this story of hope. All agents of Good and all previous prayer warriors were working overtime to see to this task.

How was this possible? I am asked this question often. I answer by saying I serve a risen Savior who came out of the grave after death. With him, all things are possible. My next book will tell of more improbable miracles and how I had my criminal record cleared. It will also tell of my fourteen years as a police officer.

Evil Never Gives Up!

Friday, July 16, 1976, was the day Kim and I were to be married in the same courthouse where I received my first drug trafficking preliminary hearing in 1973. We were to be married by the same blind judge who sat on the bench that day. This was not a coincidence. Instead, it was another appearance of the hand of our Lord. Judge Carey Warner would also play positive roles in my life for years to follow as a friend. He was indeed at my crossroads when I needed a guide.

Our wedding in 1976 (we eloped),
Just before our wedding, 1975, In our new home, 1977.

Now comes a part of this story I kept from Kim for years. An hour before our wedding, I found myself parked just a few feet from the infamous Back Row. Why was I there? A moment of weakness, for sure. It was in the middle of the day when no one was ever there. I watched as two stunning girls I had never seen before came walking toward me. They walked right up to my window, showed me a bag of pot, and asked if I wanted to party with them!

I was to be married in an hour. Who could this have been? Was it two Fallen Angels sent to rob me of my future once again? During my life on the Back Row, I would not have recognized their Evil. Today, I know this was exactly who they were. They were powerful agents from hell sent to distract my family and me from the future we now have. They were sirens sent to tempt me away from my destiny.

Without permission, they opened the door, got in, and fired up some joints. I must admit this almost worked. Somehow I managed to get out of the car and insist they get out and leave, and they did. I looked away briefly, and when I looked back in their direction, they both were gone! You can make your own determinations as to who they were. I know they were unearthly Opposing Agents from hell. Our Lord had another plan for the ladies in my life.

Kim Lemmons Stewart & Melanie Stewart Henson are just a couple of the beauties that bless me today.

Yes, I have seen Heavenly Angels take on human form to intercede for me, but on July 16, 1976, I saw the opposite. Those girls were demons right out of hell. They were sent to stop my marriage to Kim and our future generations from positively influencing the world around them. Intercession worked that day for many and not just me. *You can also measure the desperate nature of attacks against us as an indicator of how much Satan fears the future of our generations to follow!*

On a side note, Kim's mother, Jewel Lemmons, has more than replaced my mother. Words can't describe the Earthly Angel she is. It took years, but Kim's father, Al Lemmons, and I became very close too. Today, he is waiting on us in glory.

Al Lemmons, Jewel Henson Lemmons

Kim's mother, Mrs. Jewel, is more than an Earthly Angel. She came into my life at just the right time. She has also provided another haven of hope for my family.

Soon after our wedding, Kim and I were blessed with our son Donald Anthony Stewart Jr. Then, thirteen months later, Melanie Heather Stewart was born. Even with such a wonderful family and the support of Mrs. Jewel, I was still not ready to return to the full service of the Lord. It wasn't until 1983 when I rejoined our Lord's active family. Since then, I have been free from drugs and alcohol and know peace and joy beyond measure. There *is* hope for the hopeless, and I am proof!

Anthony, Tony, Zoie, Kim, Cara & Emma Stewart

Melanie Henson, Jewel Kittrell, Patrick Henson

In the battles between heaven and earth, omniscience only exists in heaven. The Fallen One can only guess at what will happen in our futures. He sees potential in us we do not see. He knows when the creator God smiles on us. He is aware of an intercessory prayer cover with our name or generation on it.

The Fallen One feared that one day I would write this story. He sent those sirens of Evil to my car before my wedding as a last resort. That last-minute drastic sneak attack failed.

Today, I pray that you or someone you care about is why I was spared to write this story. This story is not for me—it is for others who also walk on the back rows of life! I have already received blessings beyond measure. I am not one of the heroes. Instead, they are the ones I write about.

One of the fantastic things about our relationship with Jesus Christ is that we owe him nothing. We can't earn his love. We will never be able to work our way into his arms. His grace saves us, not our work! Those heroes in my life wanted to honor him with their efforts. They knew that results were not required and could never equal his sacrifice. They respect him so much they have goals to love others. Our way of showing love is sometimes only through prayer.

The heroes in my book went above and beyond and touched my life. I write to extend this touch to you. You can extend the same to someone who has lost hope as I did at different times in my life.

If Christ does not require our perfection or work, then how do we become Christians? The answer is so simple that many people miss it because they assume they must work to earn such a gift. We also lose some souls to hell because they have become too logical. They require proof of Jesus, his crucifixion, and his rise from the grave! They also over-analyze the Bible and look for errors. They use logic instead of faith. Proof does exist but only comes *after* faith.

Here is the doorway to salvation: Believe in the Lord Jesus. Believe he is risen from the grave, and ask him to forgive your sins and accept you into his arms. That's it—no work required!

Immediately, you get an eternal gift from Jesus. You are saved—period! Will you sin again? Oh yes, and often. Always pray for the forgiveness of recent sins, but you are still headed to eternal paradise even if you die before the next time you pray.

Another resource that comes to you immediately after your salvation is the Holy Spirit. He becomes a constant companion. The Holy Spirit is the source of my inspiration to write this book.

Some people find it hard to accept free will as an answer to a lot of the why questions. Understand this response: The creator God gave us all free will. He wanted us to all be different. Free will met that goal, but with that gift also came the ability not to choose him! Free will and pride disqualified Satan and other Fallen Angels in heaven from his presence. They are here among us instead.

You can choose to ignore Jesus or not believe in him. The answers to many why questions start with understanding free will.

Finally, once Jesus is your Lord, he will often send you a wave of his hand and show his presence in beautiful ways. He will use people, songs, books, and many other ways to let you see a glimpse of his hand, and those become your proof.

Let me share a wave of his hand that happened to me two times while writing this book. To set the scene, most every morning when I awake, I stay in bed to pray. I call names out to our Lord. I call out needs. I even ask for some wants. Often, I ramble, but occasionally, I see more clearly there is a specific need that requires prayer. A straightforward thought like that is directly from Jesus.

Once I am out of bed, I read God's Word before the busy day starts. Occasionally, my daily reading addresses the exact thoughts I heard from Jesus in my morning prayer time, and that's no coincidence.

I like to put on Christian music and let random songs play when I write. Once, I was writing about times when mercy was granted to me through intercessory prayers. In the middle of writing about it, the song that came on again was "Mercy Walked In" by Gordon Mote!

This morning as I am writing about salvation being a gift of mercy from the Lord Jesus, guess what song came on again? "Mercy Walked In" by Gordon Mote! Thank you, Lord, for waving your hand once again.

There was a time when I admitted to hating my life. I fell into so many *Trouble Traps* that I became miserable. For a lot of those years, I battled unhappiness. I chose a bad path resulting in much pain, and then did drugs and alcohol to drown my misery.

Today, however, I am exactly where I want to be, doing exactly what I want to do, with precisely the people I choose to do it with!

I was once hopeless, but now I have peace that goes beyond hope!

One last word of advice: Today, I spot attacks against my family and me much more effortlessly. I am often suspicious of the smallest of things, but I am not paranoid. Instead, my peace is strengthened because I know the final battle is already won. This knowledge also brings joy!

The competitive spirit I learned from my Gambrell cousins, life coaches, sports coaches, and Grandpa Lee is well used these days. I see victories all around me, and I did not have to fight for them. That is happiness, and you can have this feeling too!

Happily *Forever* After

My story is not over, but I already know what lies ahead. It would be easy to get lost in all the sadness and Evil that I described, but that is not my aim. These events are told to illustrate just how far I fell before true peace, hope, and joy were found. As a result of my Savior, Jesus Christ, I will live happily *forever* after. Please join me!

Kim & Tony Stewart 2020

I am about to finish book 2 of this series and plan on writing more books. One will be about my experiences in the world of the wealthy and famous as a smart house consultant. Each book will be filled with miracles of many types!

With that said, let me give thanks to my heroes.

My Heroes

There is no way I can list all my heroes. Some will be mentioned in other books. Others were silent influencers of whose impact I was not even aware. For all these heroes, let me say this book is about their impact. I know how to write this guide because of what each of them taught me! Please continue to pray it forward!

Families

Kim Lemmons Stewart, her mother Jewel Henson Lemmons, her father Al Lemmons, and all three brothers. All the Henson Aunts, Uncles & Cousins. Our children and grandchildren: Our son Donald (Anthony) Stewart Jr. and his wife Cara Strait Stewart; our daughter Melanie Stewart Henson, Patrick Henson, grand-children include Colin Kittrell, Jewel Kittrell, Zoie Stewart, Emma Stewart. And my first son-in-law Mr. Chris Kittrell. Thank you for your in-person and future Blessings.

My father and mother: Harry Donald Stewart and Betty Gambrell Stewart.

My grandparents: John Harrison Stewart, Blanch Charity Stewart Lee, Ellis Gambrell, LuVadie Gambrell, Mr. Oscar Lee, and all of their ancestors for past blessings and intercessory prayer cover.

My Aunt Audrey Stewart Rector. It is impossible to list all the intercession that came through this prayer warrior. Thanks to her children and especially Mary Ann, Sharon, and their brother Dan.

Thanks to the Stewart, Rector, Glenn, Gambrell, Henson, Lemmons, and other families and their previous ancestors. And a special thanks to the mighty prayer warrior Roger Henson!

Teachers, Crossing Guards, and Life Coaches

Mr. Smiley Williams, Mrs. Harper, Mrs. Margaret Bull, Mrs. Kathryn Harrington and her daughter Candi and husband Randy Vaughn, Mr. Chip Sloan, School Counselor Mary Hayes, Nurse Nelly Gordon, Mimi Gordon, Gigi, and Didi Gordon.

Chris and Linda Wood Dumas, Judy O., and Robbie M.

Sports Coaches: Steve Gambrell, Billy White, Riley Jones, Butch Miller, and Robert Gillespie.

Victor United Methodist Church

Minister Phil Jones and family.

SC Trooper McCrary

Mount Lebanon Baptist Church

Mr. Smiley Williams, Mr. Chip Sloan (again), and the entire congregation.

Mrs. Georgia Sloan.

Pastor Delano McMinn and Wilene.

Pastor Scott McAlister.

Music Minister Ted Conwell and Debbie.

The athletes who invited me to play for Mt. Lebanon teams.

Strong Leaders & Friends

Dr. Jack Davis and Phyllis

Mentor and Electronics Supervisor Dan Eubanks, Supervisor Richard Bailey

Greenville County Deputy Gary Gilstrap & Bonnie

And a special thanks to long-time mentors Pastor Mark Smith and Freida

God bless you all!

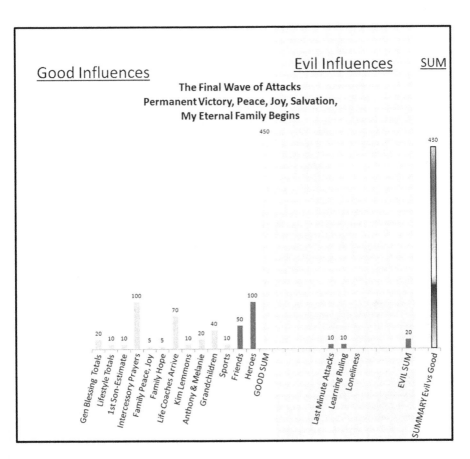

The battles continue, but eternal peace, hope, and joy will remain.

CPSIA information can be obtained
at www.ICGtesting.com
Printed in the USA
LVHW080553160322
713572LV00003B/244